'Stuart Buchanan's ability to draw psychology, sociology, theology, and and recruitment is to be highly co~~mmended. It is great to~~ ~~finally~~ see a book which offers those involved in discerning vocation a full toolkit for the task.'

Margaret Sentamu, Head of Diversity, Odgers Ray & Berndtson, former Senior Selection Secretary, Church of England

'The many years of experience which Stuart brings together in this book make it a must-have resource for all those involved in interviewing and helping Christians to explore their calling. His honest and thorough handling of the subject recognizes that the process can be complex and painstaking but also a joy and a privilege. The combination of godly insight, real-life stories, practical tools and sometimes painful experience all reflect a heart to see God's people become the right people in the right place at the right time.'

Jo Jowett, Associate Director, Christian Vocations

'Helping others to discern God's call is an incredible privilege and an awesome responsibility. This book is an essential tool for those who walk with someone in the journey of vocation discovery. It is full of fascinating insights, useful information and practical wisdom. It will both enlighten and equip. I warmly commend this immensely helpful handbook for all who are involved in a process of interview and selection.'

Bishop Ken Clarke, Chairperson of the Church of Ireland Bishops' Selection Conference

After working in mission in inner-city Britain and rural Kenya, Stuart Buchanan worked for nearly 30 years for the Church Mission Society encouraging, nurturing and testing vocation for mission service. For the last 15 years, he has been involved in training interviewers for a number of different mission agencies as well as training those who select clergy. This work has taken him not only to the UK and Ireland but also to Nigeria, Kenya, Singapore and Korea.

Stuart Buchanan then worked in the Mission and Evangelism Department of the Anglican Communion Office researching and preparing material for the 2008 Lambeth Conference, and as a freelance consultant and trainer. He is a licensed Reader in the Anglican Diocese of Southwark and is the author of *On Call* (BRF, 2001).

CALLED BY GOD?

A handbook for those testing Christian vocation

STUART BUCHANAN

First published in Great Britain in 2008

Society for Promoting Christian Knowledge
36 Causton Street
London SW1P 4ST

British Library Cataloguing-in-Publication Data
A catalogue record for this book is available from the British Library

ISBN 978–0–281–06052–8

1 3 5 7 9 10 8 6 4 2

Typeset by Graphicraft Ltd, Hong Kong
Printed in Great Britain by Ashford Colour Press

Produced on paper from sustainable forests

Contents

Contents

Part 3
BEFORE INTERVIEWING

Part 4
INTERVIEWING

Contents

Part 5
MAKING DECISIONS

Introduction

There's a story told of a management consultant's report produced for Jesus, giving him an assessment of his chosen 12 disciples. The consultant begins by ruling out Peter, as being too impetuous, always speaking or acting first and thinking afterwards; Thomas is seen as lacking trust and asking too many questions; James and John are dismissed as poor team players who are full of their own importance. Using the language of human resources, the report lists many of the faults, vulnerabilities, weaknesses and fragilities of 11 of the disciples before going on to conclude that the only reliable disciple is Judas Iscariot! Obviously, Jesus did not use modern HR criteria when he chose his disciples.

Two thousand years later, Christians still believe that the God revealed in Jesus has tasks and roles for his followers and that somehow he encourages them and gives them the strength to take on these tasks. All Christians, through their baptism into the Body of Christ, have a calling or vocation to be involved in the work and mission of God, but the Church and its agencies have created specific types of ministry for which it is essential that there are criteria and processes to discern and test a possible vocation to that ministry.

My opening story makes it clear that God's ways are not humanity's ways and that testing someone's vocation to a particular ministry may be a very different process from that of appointing someone to a secular position. Some of these differences are:

- In the secular world, selection usually begins with the writing of a job description. From this, a person specification is drawn up, stating which attributes are essential and which are desirable. The post is then advertised and the post offered to the applicant who best matches the person specification. In contrast, the roles and attributes covered by the term 'vocation' often cannot be defined neatly within such a job description and person specification.
- Generally, vocational processes are not competitive; traditionally 'The harvest is plentiful, but the labourers are few' (Matt. 9.37), which means there are usually far more openings than people to fill them. In the secular job market, it is possible to affirm unsuccessful candidates by telling them that although they were good, someone else was better. In vocational interviews people are likely to be in competition only with themselves. Not only can this make selection harder, as it is about

absolute standards rather than about the best candidate, but it also makes the task of saying 'no' to candidates potentially more hurtful. We can cope with hearing that 'someone else was better', but it is harder to hear that 'you were not good enough'.

- The national press takes very little interest in Christian vocation until there is a scandal. These occasional, but high-profile, revelations in the press are a reminder that vocation is not usually about a nine-to-five, five-days-a-week job; it is about the whole of a person's life. It will be essential not only to explore how well the person can 'do the job' but also whether that vocation is integrated into the rest of his or her life so that it affirms, rather than damages, the ability to live out the vocation. All this means that issues need to be explored that are not generally explored within secular job interviews.

- Most vocations involve longer than usual working hours and require the need to make sacrifices that will have an impact upon the wider family. Some vocations must involve a call on both husband and wife, but with any vocation there are likely to be issues about how the vocation should be perceived and owned within the wider family and how this is explored.

- In an attempt to avoid 'the ways of the world', it can be easy for vocation-testing processes to spiritualize issues and not do justice to them.

- Many Christian agencies are small and those testing vocation can find that they already know a candidate or the candidate's family, making objectivity difficult.

- The concept of Christian vocation includes an understanding that in some way God has revealed his mind, both to the candidate and the selectors. Post-modern thinking questions the concept of such revelation; this leads to ambiguities and tensions in the way in which people might feel comfortable expressing their understanding of such revelation. In particular, there can be considerable difference in the language of vocation between those exploring their vocation and those testing it.

- Testing vocation does not just include a match of skills and experience; it will also consider how the candidate can reach his or her full potential in Christ.

- Traditionally, vocation has been seen as something that is for life. Looking at many of the traditional vocations, and trying to imagine what they will look like in 20 or 30 years, challenges the imagination. Some may cease to exist, or will have changed beyond recognition. Increasingly people are seeing their life made up of a series of short-term 'vocations' or as a long-term vocation to a series of changing ministries. How do we test vocation against this background?

- Although a vocation has always been seen as something that grows over a period of time, we live in a world where people seek the instant, and the immediate.
- Many of those who explore their vocation can be devastated when their offer to serve is not accepted. This can lead to them being seriously damaged pastorally and spiritually, and so being very unlikely to reach their full potential in Christ in the near future.

This book draws on my own experience of having interviewed mission personnel on behalf of the Church Mission Society (CMS) for 27 years, encouraging, nurturing and testing vocation. I have also been fortunate to take part in numerous diocesan and national vocation events, which have enabled me to gain a good overview of the types of ministries of the Church and its agencies. It also draws on my experience of training interviewers, in England, Ireland, Nigeria, Kenya, Singapore and Korea, both for the selection of mission personnel for various mission agencies as well as for the selection of clergy. Often the training has raised questions for the participants about their selection procedures and I have been privileged to gain insights into different selection criteria and processes. Different organizations, rightly, have different selection criteria and processes, taking different periods of time and employing different methods, but there are certain underlying principles that should be common to most explorations of vocation.

Here, I start by considering how vocation is understood at the beginning of the twenty-first century, before going on to consider what we are trying to achieve through our selection processes and the tools that we have at our disposal as we formulate our selection strategy. I then go on to consider different issues related to interviewing. I conclude by considering what to do with the information that has been gathered, the range of decisions available and how decisions can be made and given.

I hope that this book will be useful for all those who are involved in encouraging, nurturing or testing vocation to different full-time or part-time Christian ministries such as clergy, authorized layministries, mission partners, youth workers or evangelists. I have provided a number of questions for reflection and you may find it helpful to engage with these, along with your fellow interviewers, as you work through the book.

Employment law is constantly changing and also it might not be clear whether a person is classed as an employee if he or she pursues a certain vocation. With this in mind, and noting that this book is written also for those living outside the UK and the European Union, readers should familiarize themselves with employment law within the country of origin and the country where they work out their calling, rather than draw legal conclusions from this book.

Part 1

WHAT IS A 'VOCATION'?

1

Understanding vocation

I was at a meeting where different agencies were discussing issues related to vocation and their selection criteria. Someone wisely commented that, with the exception of the need for a vocation to that ministry, the other criteria were those that we would expect to find within many mature Christians. It might seem obvious but this does mean that a vocation to a particular ministry needs to be the first criterion.

But what do different people mean by the word 'vocation'? In the past there were broadly accepted ways of expressing vocation within the different parts of the Church. There were common vocabularies of vocation and less need to delve deeper and discover the meaning beneath the words; this is no longer true.

In order to test vocation, it will be essential to have a grasp of what vocation is and of the diversity of understanding that might be encompassed by the word. It is helpful to consider a range of understandings, or models, of vocation. I refer to several books on the subject, all written from different perspectives. In choosing particular references, I cannot hope to do justice to any of them, and each of them offers far more insights than I am able to refer to here. There is a danger that, although I read widely, I might still quote narrowly!

Reflect . . .

Before proceeding, take a moment to ask yourself these questions:

- How do you understand the term 'vocation'?
- What issues do you feel will determine how a person understands his or her vocation?
- What influences the vocabulary people use to describe their sense of call?

The following chapters will help you to explore these questions further.

What is meant by 'vocation'?

All Christians are vocational people

All Christians have, or should have, a vocation through being baptized in Christ. Part of the task of all Christians is to discover and live out their personal vocation. This may or may not include the types of vocation that the Church or its agencies need to test. Paul reminds us in 1 Corinthians 12 that this does not mean that such callings are worthier than others; it just means that their nature is different, and each relies upon the others as part of the Body of Christ.

Francis Dewar in his book *Called or Collared?*[1] helpfully describes three distinct ways in which the terms 'vocation' or 'calling' are used.

- There is the general sense of God's calling to everyone to be a follower of Christ and to become a member of his body, the Church.
- There is the understanding of a calling to a role. A role is essentially something defined by others. The call to a role is not for everyone.
- The third sense of the word refers to a person's unique or personal vocation.

> Potentially this again is for everyone. By it I mean a task or activity engaged in for the love of it by which others may be enriched or released: something you do as a freely-chosen expression of your nature and energy, something that expresses the unique essence of yourself which God calls out from you to be a gift to others . . . It is something that you will feel as it were from within, as an inner urge or prompting.

This book considers the second understanding of vocation – a call to a specific type of ministry – but, as Francis Dewar goes on to suggest, these are roles that are filled by people who have the third understanding of vocation. Confusion and pain can arise when Christians, experiencing the third kind of understanding, believe that their vocation can only be fulfilled within a ministry that belongs to the second understanding of vocation and yet they are turned down for such roles.

All Christians, as part of the Body of Christ, have a responsibility to help other members of the Body to understand the different ways in which vocation can be outworked and to encourage and nurture vocation. In the New Testament, the first example of the wider Body of Christ discerning vocation is described in Acts 6. In *On Call*[2] I note that in the task of choosing seven deacons from the Hellenist community, the Hebrew apostles first draw up guidelines, then delegate the task of selection to the local Hellenist community, then prayerfully affirm the selection process and ordain the chosen deacons. In Acts 13, the Holy Spirit directs the church in Antioch to set aside Barnabas and Saul for certain tasks; the same Holy Spirit still prompts the Church and its agencies to prayerfully set aside people for specific tasks and ministry.

Journey and growth

I was once asked to give a talk about the 'hurdles that folk needed to jump to get through CMS selection processes'. I didn't find it a very helpful title, and spoke instead on vocation as a journey. Sometimes we set off on a journey not really sure of where we are going, but open to be guided en route. Journeys need to be at the right speed; the fable of the tortoise and the hare reminds us that those who start too fast might tire and not complete the journey, whereas those who are slower and more patient will have the stamina to get there. Sometimes there will be deviations and detours and time well spent on the journey. As an interviewer I would sometimes see my responsibility as giving a green light, but sometimes a red, or a left filter or an amber – proceed with caution.

God calls people to do tasks for him; the word 'call' appears 167 times in the Bible (NRSV). However, there are many people who carry out tasks for God where the word 'call' is not mentioned in the text. If someone is moving in the right direction, he or she doesn't need the divine nudge in the way that the person who is static or moving in the wrong direction does. Abram is recognized as the first person called by God and is seen as an example of stepping out in faith on a journey. We read at the end of Genesis 11 that the journey from Ur to Canaan was actually started by Abraham's father, Terah; he stopped when he got as far as Haran, and Abram finished the journey.[3]

I have often interviewed those completing a Master's degree that was preparing them to work overseas, rather than in the UK; they had already begun their journey. I interviewed a lady who, after spending her first 16 years of life in East Africa, had subsequently returned there in her early 20s. She was aged nearly 50 when I interviewed her and had spent over two-thirds of her life in East Africa. For such a person, the divine nudge would be needed to not work overseas, but to work in the UK.

Although Abram was completing a journey that his father began and that was probably part of wider migration around the Fertile Crescent, what set him apart from others making that journey was that he believed that God had wanted him to do so. We may find ourselves testing the vocation of those who have already begun a journey, and who need God to stop or redirect them, but I would suggest that, like Abram, they should still be able to articulate in some way where God is in the journey and the process.

In her spiritual work *Landmarks*,[4] Margaret Silf introduces us to some of the insights of St Ignatius Loyola; 'consolation' is the term used when our underlying heart journey is focused on God and drawn towards him, and 'desolation' is when that heart journey is drifting away from God. Her book honestly recognizes that our spiritual journey will include both experiences. Ignatius concluded: 'When in desolation, don't take life-changing decisions, and don't go back on a decision that you took during a period of consolation.'[5] This is helpfully illustrated with the example of a narrow boat going through a winding canal tunnel. At times there might be no light from either the entrance or the exit, but it is impossible to turn the narrow boat around in the tunnel, nor can it successfully be steered backwards! The only course is to go onwards until the light from the exit is discovered.[6]

Often at vocation and debriefing conferences, I have invited people to draw a 'time-line', mapping out the highs and lows of their experiences over a particular period of time. Having done this, it can be helpful to draw another line on the graph to indicate how close God appeared to be at different times, particularly during the highs and lows. It can also be worth considering that, if the distance changes, who has moved – God or you? This can be a helpful way of beginning a self-exploration of times of consolation and desolation.

Motivation and five ways not to spell 'vocation'

I sometimes think that people have trouble spelling the word 'vocation'. Perhaps my examples relate more to the sending of people to other countries, but I feel that they still have some relevance for other forms of vocation. I have come across people who seem to spell 'vocation' in the following ways.

1 **Vacation** – a romantic and unrealistic view of the vocation in question, a sense of holiday from the reality of everyday life;
2 **Location** – a desire to go to a particular place, and a vocation could be the way of achieving the visa and ticket;
3 **Vacancy** – an awareness of a need and a matching of skills for the task, but no understanding beyond a strictly functional one;
4 **Vacuum** – a sense of trying to fill an emptiness that is left by something, someone or a real relationship with God, being missing;
5 **Vacate** – an attempt to run away from a relationship, failure, reality or from oneself or God.

I was rather thrown one time when presenting my five misspellings to be asked whether they can legitimately be part of the calling. Although I wanted to answer no, I am sure that the true answer is yes. We are fallen and contain a mass of contradictions. God can and does still use us despite our mixed motives; the wrong motive may well be the starting point that God needs to address during the testing and discernment process. The important point is that an unaddressed wrong motive must not be allowed to be the dominant motivation as the process evolves.

'If God's called me, it won't be a problem'

Sometimes when I have interviewed people, and am exploring a particular issue, they have responded by stating that if God is calling them then he will take care of that particular issue and it will not be a problem. How can I disagree with this conclusion? To do so might suggest that I do not have such a depth of faith in God. An even worse conclusion is the implication that I work for a Christian organization that is so unspiritual as to employ someone like myself who has voiced doubt in what God can do. Instead I will agree with them, but rephrase their conclusion by saying, 'Yes, I agree. If I can find evidence that this issue is unlikely to be a problem, then God may be calling you.'

Finding the right person

In his book *How to Find Your Vocation*,[7] John Adair suggests that
people who are likely to discover their vocation share certain characteristics. He liberates vocation from the narrowing confines of a
Christian understanding and offers the following list, not with the
assumption that every vocational person will have each characteristic,
but rather that there are core characteristics that will be found
within his list:

- dedication or commitment;
- fitness – how well interests, aptitude and temperament are in
  balance with the needs and requirement of the work;
- not for money alone – the motivation is not dependent upon
  financial reward;
- creativity;
- enthusiasm – the sense of the work being a source of enjoyment
  and fun, and the sense of passion for the work;
- humility – a sense of the work being larger and more important
  than the person doing it;
- tenacity;
- service – a sense of being motivated to help or serve others; and
- love of the work.

For many Christian vocations I would wish to add to Adair's list
both being a team player and being an enabler.

The vocational pyramid

In the 'Fit for the Purpose' weekend vocation conferences run by
the Extension Studies Department of St John's College, Nottingham,
which are based upon the *Fit for the Purpose* workbook,[8] participants are encouraged to use a tool described as a vocational pyramid. The workbook suggests three types of calling: the call to Adam
and Eve, to live out their humanity in God's world; the call to
Abraham and his family, to belong to God as his people, a people
of faith; the call to Moses, to serve God and bring his people free-
dom. Participants in the weekend vocation conferences are encouraged to consider their humanity as the base of the pyramid; built
on this is their faith. God, like a crane completing a tall building,
then lowers their task or vocation as the top of the pyramid onto
the foundations that they have built.

Within the workbook, a model is presented in which each level of the pyramid is divided into six attributes, so that strengths and weaknesses within each level can be explored. The base needs to be strong enough to bear the weight of the task. If the weight of the task is placed over an area of weakness, the whole pyramid may collapse, damaging both the faith and humanity that lie below. Sadly, some people will attempt to seek a vocation that compensates for a weakness within their humanity or faith. The exercise increases self-awareness in understanding participants' strengths and weaknesses. This in turn allows them both to explore a vocation that builds upon their strengths, and to explore what work needs to be done to address weaknesses and vulnerabilities.

This model also stresses the importance of having appropriate boundaries between the three levels. On the one hand, there is a danger that the three will be blurred together: it is inappropriate to be meeting some of your human needs through your vocation. It is also very easy for those with a vocation to find that their spiritual life is primarily fed by their sermon preparation, Bible study preparation or writing, rather than their spiritual life feeding into their ministry. While blurring the three layers together is not good for either a healthy physical or spiritual life, on the other hand there is also a danger if these three areas are lived in total isolation from each other. It is important that those with a vocation can 'walk the talk' and that their everyday life, lived out at the human level, is consistent with what is expected of their vocation and doesn't compromise their witness. Each level must inform and interact with the other layers.

Expectations and reality

Many people may be very aware of God's call on their lives as the starting point in exploring their vocation. What they may not be so aware of is all of the other factors that are influencing how they perceive that sense of calling and the range of assumptions and expectations that they take with them into the discernment process. During this process their different assumptions and expectations need to be converged or melded so that they fit the reality of the actual vocation. Of course, this process takes place not only through the different stages of selection, but also through the training processes and through the matching of candidates with appropriate locations or openings within their particular ministry.

External factors may also influence a candidate's expectations. For example, when the Church of England began to ordain women as priests, women had a new vocation that they could explore, and fewer women explored overseas service. Realities may also change for an organization; financial constraints may mean that fewer candidates can be accepted than you would like. When exploring vocation it is important to try to match the candidate's expectations with the reality that your organization offers.

It's worth remembering that people's expectations can only be changed a certain amount and sometimes the selection process will need to flag up the candidate's assumptions and expectations as unrealistic.

Family considerations

If someone is married then it is important to make sure that both partners feel a sense of calling, particularly in the case of overseas work. Although at times one partner within a marriage may feel a sense of God's leading to overseas work, most mission agencies believe that 'What therefore God hath joined together, let not man put asunder' (Matt. 19.6, av). They are unlikely to send just one partner overseas for any substantial length of time, but would want to engage with both husband and wife equally. Most mission agencies would see the vocation as something that would be shared and affirmed, although perhaps in different ways, by both partners.

Although overseas mission provides an extreme example of the impact of a person's vocation on other family members, any type of ministry that is defined as a vocation is likely to make demands beyond normal working hours, and may determine where people need to live and how they are viewed within the local community. Although the vocation may be seen as belonging to only one part-ner of a marriage, it does need to be affirmed, encouraged and enabled by the other partner and by their children. As such, consideration needs to be given as to how this affirmation, encour-agement and enabling is viewed, valued and explored.

When is vocation likely?

In the concluding chapter of *On Call*,[9] I suggest that there are four ways in which God can move someone and that, in the twenty-first century, vocation is likely when all four come together. Although written from the perspective of cross-cultural mission, I would suggest that they still apply to other forms of ministry. There will need to be:

- a task to be done, and the skills and gifts to match the task;
- an ability to learn and grow within a new setting;
- a sense of obedience to God's leading; and
- a sense of being a representative, chosen and prayerfully supported by some part of the Body of Christ.

Exploring potential

At vocational events I sometimes pretend to interview some of the early saints. In response to my questions, I project an appropriate passage of scripture upon the screen behind me: I ask Peter about the first time someone asked if he knew Jesus, and project the reference to his three-fold denial; Paul is asked about his early contact with Christians, and a reference to the story of Stephen's martyrdom is projected; Mark is asked about his short-term placement with Paul and Barnabas, and a reference to his early return is projected. I then make the audience aware of some of the amazing things that these fallen and vulnerable people were able to achieve for the Kingdom.

The references to Paul and Mark are a reminder of the key role of Barnabas in enabling both of them to fulfil their vocation. Barnabas is the one who is able to recognize potential and trust and to nurture those that others would reject.[10] Some of the people I have interviewed for long-term service are those I interviewed for short-term service many years ago. On occasions, the pattern of service is reversed; those who returned from long-term service, because of the needs of their children or their parents, then considered further service after they had been freed of the responsibilities of their families. Often I was in a position of being able to remember people as they had been. This had its advantages, but also its limitations; if I was trapped in seeing them as they had been, was I able to see them as they now were?

An awareness of how people have moved on, and grown and changed over the years, helps me to the next stage of trying to imagine people as they might be. I am sure that Christ tries to see us as we might be; to see the potential that we might have if we continue in relationship with him and open ourselves to his healing touch within our lives. The task of helping people discover their vocation is not just to see what they can offer now but, without losing sight of what has been and what is, to see what might be and to try to help people to realize that possibility.[11]

Ironically, if we ever find a candidate who has reached his or her full potential then we should not accept that person, who is no longer able to grow! We only need to look at the 12 disciples that Jesus chose to realize that he was not just taking them at face value, but seeking to understand the potential that was there. Most Christian vocations offer training to those that they accept and this should be the first step in helping them to make the most of their gifts and abilities. It is still unlikely to bring them to their full potential, but will, it is to be hoped, give them the tools to enable them to keep working towards it.

> **Reflect . . .**
>
> What impact do different understandings of vocation have on how vocation should be explored? What issues should be explored when testing vocation? (Some suggestions are included in Chapter 5.)

2

Developing vocation

Reflect . . .

Is vocation an instantaneous gift from God, or does it grow?

In Matthew 25.14–30, Jesus tells the parable of the talents, in which God is like the master and we are the servants. All of us are given talents that God expects us to use for the Kingdom. If we use them, they grow; if we fail to use them, they are taken away from us. The discovery, growth and use of such talents should be part of each Christian's self-discovery and discipleship. Sometimes this self-discovery and growth will be confused with a vocation to a specific type of ministry. Certainly those with such a vocation will be those who have an awareness of their talents and who are able to use them and make them grow for the Kingdom, but there will be a need for more than a purely functional understanding of vocation. Just as talents are grown over a period of time, so vocation needs to be grown.

The argument for gradual growth

Someone was describing to me his vocation to join the Church Army, 35 years previously. He had shared his sense of leading with his vicar, who told him to come back and speak with him again in a year's time; if the vocation was real it would grow, if it was not real it would diminish. I can't imagine any vicar saying that to a member of his or her congregation today, but the point that the vicar was making is still a valid and important one.

The late Lesslie Newbigin, writing in 1984,[12] looks at the emphasis in our culture on the instant rather than on growth. In particular he pointed to the emphasis on gifts of the Spirit rather than on fruit of the Spirit. Jesus' teaching is set within a rural setting where people were familiar with the fact that to grow wheat, vines or a fig tree not only took time, but there was also the need for much careful work if the crop was to be produced. Despite the fact that his formative years would be shaped by Joseph being involved in carpentry, Jesus' analogies depended more upon agriculture and slow growth.

Our world is shaped more by industrial society, where items are produced very rapidly and we expect instant results. Even within agricultural produce we speak of factory chickens and genetically modified crops. Our industrial society has even speeded up how long vegetables need to grow; no longer do we wait for 'our fruit in due season', but force it to grow in greenhouses, or fly it in from a country where it is in season. Understandably, Lesslie Newbigin argued, with this mindset when we think of the Holy Spirit we prefer to think of gifts that are instant, rather than fruit that takes time and much cultivation.

This thinking readily transfers to the issue of vocation. Even given how our differing cultural understandings have an impact on our interpretation of Scripture, and how our generational perspectives affect our outlook, vocation is still something that needs to be grown and nurtured over time.

For many, the Christian journey will be a time of gradual growth into a closer relationship with God; others, perhaps in response to particular circumstances, will experience times when they are aware of a period of rapid spiritual growth. Such experiences can easily be confused with vocation.

One of my early vocational choices was leaving industry to work with people, and a stimulus to this decision was finding that as a concerned Christian in industry I had helped to conclude that it was better to throw away our chemical effluent, rather than recycle it. I can now easily accuse myself of choosing the easier option; the tough vocation might have been to live out my life as a Christian concerned about the environment within that particular industry. I can think of others who, having been accepted for a Christian ministry, have commented that no one asked why they wanted to leave their previous job. To wrestle honestly and fully with our own motives takes time and cannot be done instantly.

Often, when people become aware of a sense of calling they can make the assumption that God is leading them to a particular role because they know others who are fulfilling their vocation within that role. Typically, when there is a sense of God's leading them to full-time Christian work, there can be an assumption that this means becoming an ordained minister; if there is a sense of God's leading them to cross-cultural mission, there can be an assumption that this is to an overseas location rather than to a multiracial, inner-city setting in one's own country. It can, and should, take time to prayerfully discover and reflect upon the different possibilities and sense God's leading in a particular direction.

I analysed the lead-in time of those who applied to CMS during a certain period. I looked at the expectations that people had of the length of time between first making contact and when they expected to begin their training. For those whose vocation was affirmed, the lead-in time was almost double that for those whose vocation was not affirmed. Obviously there could be various reasons for such a discrepancy, but we concluded that those expecting a faster lead-in time had not thought through their sense of vocation as thoroughly as those who anticipated a longer one.

Initial interviews, within selection processes, are unlikely just to 'test' vocation; they are also likely to stimulate thought. Interview questions are not neutral instruments merely measuring the vocational temperature at a point in time. A good question (see p. 136) can be the stimulus that opens up possibilities. Often at this stage in the process we will want to leave candidates with some specific questions to reflect upon and, perhaps, some suggested reading or gaining of experience to broaden their perspectives; again, this takes time.

Most people who have been accepted for a particular Christian ministry will, at some point within that ministry, have times of doubt as to whether their calling was real. What often keeps people going at such times, giving them a sense of assurance and peace of mind, is the knowledge that the sense of vocation was something that grew over a period of time, rather than being a whim.

Having your vocation tested too soon, if it means that your vocation is not affirmed, can be a devastating experience. Although, at one level, candidates should be going into the selection process trusting the selectors to discern God's will and discover what is best for them, it is never as simple as that. In order to do justice to your-self and to God, at the final stage of a selection process you do need to believe that God is calling you. Then to be told 'no' can be very confusing and damaging, not only to the person concerned but also to the congregation that has supported a candidate through this process. Although there are many examples where such an answer has been the stimulus for growth, testing vocation too soon can easily result in stunting the growth completely.

In the chapter on the subject of growth in *On Call*,[13] I conclude 'that growth needs to be taking place at all levels – within our understanding of our calling; in the gaining of relevant talents and experiences; in self-awareness; in biblical understanding; in rela-tionship with God and in relationship to the community where the calling will be lived out'.

Encouraging, nurturing or testing vocation?

Reflect . . .

Do you only 'test' vocation or are you also involved in encouraging and nurturing vocation? How do you view the differences between these roles?

Even after 20 years, I still have embarrassing memories of a talk I gave to a university group. I was meant to be encouraging vocation, and I am sure that what I had prepared would have been appro-priate for this. However, just before the talk I was asked to chat to someone about his sense of vocation. For various reasons he seemed totally inappropriate for cross-cultural mission, but he was going to be part of the group that I was to address. I ended up aiming my talk at that person, rather than the rest of the group. Basically I had switched from encouraging vocation to testing vocation.

There are very different roles involved in encouraging, nurturing and testing vocation; often the people who are good at one will be good at the other tasks because there needs to be the same under-standing of vocation within all three, but we need to be careful that we know which role we are meant to be fulfilling at a particular time. Often encouraging will be something that we do with a group of people; it might involve some small-group activities but in the main it will be a one-way flow of information from us to our listeners. It is good to encourage people to talk about issues with each other or to be involved in exercises, but we will not be engaging deeply with the answers. We will be opening up possibilities and encouraging thought, prayer and further discussion.

Nurturing vocation has many of the tasks of gardening; it will involve digging, stimulating growth and pruning. We are likely to be acting in a counselling role, which can involve us in much digging for information, helping the person to explore his or her self-awareness and other issues more deeply and to reflect upon the options. If there is not a vocation to the ministry of our agency, we should be helping the person to discover this for himself or herself. We, and our organizations, should be better able to cope with people 'rejecting' us than they will be with us 'rejecting' them. When the nurturer, and the person concerned, feel that the time is right, the process should move from nurturing to testing.

As the mode has changed it can help the process if the task of testing vocation is handled by a different person from the nurturing. When you nurture vocation, you will usually want to see that vocation affirmed and it is important that the process becomes more objective at the testing stage. Within selection for the ministry, the local or diocesan process will usually pass a candidate on to a national process at this point. Similarly, for most mission agencies, the actual testing of vocation is conducted by those who are not staff, but by a more objective group of interviewers who are better able to hear what God is saying rather than, more subjectively, responding to the needs of the individual or the needs of the location.

Vocational conferences

There are vocational events run nationally and locally; some can be aimed at those exploring a particular type of ministry and others should present a variety of types of Christian vocation. They can be very helpful for a number of reasons.

- Usually, particularly with a national conference, there is a sense of anonymity and the enquirer will not be known by those running the conference, which takes away some pressures; it is an opportunity to begin to explore vocation without building up the expectations of others; you are not beginning a process that might suck you along to the next stage.

- The conference will present information that is helpful for the enquirer to begin to reflect upon his or her sense of God's leading and suggest further exercises or resources.

- It can be very helpful to any enquirer to meet others who are beginning to explore their vocation as well. Apart from making such an exploration appear more normal, the conference can be an opportunity to engage with the questions of the other enquirers, as well as the answers of those presenting the information.

- Many conferences will open up the options of different types of ministry so that objective decisions can be made about the options.

- Weekend conferences, rather than day events, can be an opportunity for objective one-to-one conversations with staff, to begin work on some personal issues and also for the mutual prayer support of the other participants.

Books

In nurturing vocation, you may wish to suggest reading and ask the candidate to reflect upon his or her understanding of certain issues, either orally at a future meeting or in writing for further discussion at another time. There are some excellent books available covering both the subject of vocation and an exploration of different ministries; some of these were mentioned in Chapter 1.

Gaining experience

This chapter began with the tension between the need for growth and the demand for the immediate. Although I remain convinced that vocation needs to be developed over time, there are experiences that can be gained 'immediately' that will help in that process of growth. Mission agencies often offer short-term experiences, perhaps for a few weeks or for between six months and two years. These experiences should be valid in their own right, but one of the purposes can be to help grow vocation.

Many who are exploring ordination are able to gain experience as lay assistants or in other ways. With most types of ministry there will be ways of gaining some type of experience that should satisfy the need for the immediate and also provide a real opportunity to engage deeply with some of the relevant experiences to help determine whether the vocation is really growing in that direction.

It is particularly important that such short-term experiences should provide an opportunity to learn outside the normal comfort zone; this is best achieved if such explorations are 'incarnational', rather than its being achieved by commuting into the proving ground every morning and commuting back to the comfort zone every evening.

In order to get the most from such experiences, it is important to build in evaluation and debriefing so that there can be proper reflection on what has been learned. My understanding has been that it is helpful to provide individual debriefing as soon as possible afterwards, followed by a corporate debriefing event, ideally two or three months later, when further reflection and evaluation has taken place. Such debriefing processes should be seen as an integral part of the experience, and not as an optional extra.

Evolving vocations

There is an assumption that although a vocation needs to be developed, once you have one the process is complete. It is hoped, however, that Christians continue to grow and this might well mean that God leads them into new and different ways of exercising their vocation. Tongue in cheek, I can say that I know several people who spent 30 years in parish ministry as a way of growing their vocation for overseas mission! In reality I know many more who spent time in cross-cultural mission as a way of growing their vocation to ordained ministry or for a lay ministry, alongside a secular job, within a multicultural, inner-city area.

In helping to develop vocation I would encourage the person to reflect upon how this particular stage in his or her vocation might tie in with God's long-term plans. For example, if a person is at a career crossroads, he or she should be helped to reflect upon whether, vocationally, the next step would be part of a journey of discovery or a cul-de-sac. So, it is all right to be 30 with a spouse and a one-year-old child and to find yourself at a crossroads within your career but if, 10 years later – now aged 40 with three children – you return from overseas because of your children's education and you are at another professional crossroads, you may find life quite difficult, and also find it difficult, in retrospect, to make sense of the previous ten years.

The question is whether vocational decisions now will open up or close down vocation possibilities in the future. It is not wrong to close down future options, but I think it is wrong for such future options to be rejected without the person realizing that he or she is making what are possibly irreversible decisions. If the vocation is unlikely to last until retirement age then it can be helpful to ask how this stage ties in with God's longer-term calling on the candidate's life. Often there will not be an easy answer, but I think that it is important that the question is asked and that any next step is considered in the light of the longer-term calling.

3

Generational issues and personality

Personality and vocation

One of the changes that I noticed over many years of interviewing is that Christians have become far more aware of their personalities: some had trained in counselling, which had involved them in much self-exploration; others had been counselled, to help them to understand and address issues. Seeking counselling has lost the stigma that it might have had 20 years ago; dealing with issues, rather than ignoring them, has become the natural thing to do.

The more we understand about personality, the more we realize that it can have an impact upon both the candidate's and our own understanding of vocation. Much psychology has been based upon a Freudian analysis that causes some difficulties for many Christians. The assumptions underlying a Jungian analysis, although still causing problems for some Christians, have generally become more acceptable. The Myers-Briggs Type Indicator, a tool that is based upon a Jungian understanding, has increasingly been used by Christians during the last 20 years. The Myers-Briggs test is not the only personality tool that Christians can use but, because many Christians are now familiar with them, they can help to make the point clearly about the link between personality and understanding of vocation.

The Myers-Briggs test considers four different personality traits ('types'). Isabel Briggs Myers and Katharine Briggs define their terminology more distinctly than I do here, but the four traits are:

- Introvert or Extrovert;
- Intuitive or Sensing;
- Feeling or Thinking;
- Judging (closing things down) or Perceiving (keeping things open).

The rationale behind Myers-Briggs is that everyone is clearly one or the other within each of these four traits. Although there is no middle ground, some people will not have a clear understanding of which they are. I believe that each of these traits can influence how we understand our vocation.

- The Introvert–Extrovert indicator is about whether the world that people inhabit is within themselves (introvert) or outside themselves (extrovert). I find that some people will sense their call as being within them, an inner leading, and others will respond to what is going on in the outside world.
- The Intuitive–Sensing indicator is about whether people understand things intuitively, going for the big picture, or whether they are sensing, and have an eye for the details. Again, this can be reflected in how people understand their vocation.
- The Feeling–Thinking indicator is connected with whether the sense of God's leading is a feeling or the result of a cerebral process.
- The Judging–Perceiving indicator is reflected in whether people have a clear-cut understanding of their sense of God's leading or are more open-ended about this.

Given that each personality trait has two options, there are 16 different personality types. Although these 16 different personality traits are not evenly distributed, the likelihood is that anyone we interview will have a different personality type from ours and will understand their vocation in a different way from the way that we will understand our own.

I remember that when my personality was assessed and explained at a workshop I had a feeling of being highly affirmed as a person. I then realized that I had exactly the same personality indicators as the person running the workshop! Despite that, the lesson that I brought away with me was that there are no right or wrong personalities; it is just that they are different.

The point that I want to make is that if the understanding of vocation comes from a person's personality, we cannot consider that one understanding is right and another one is wrong; each is equally valid. The differences are all part of God's rich tapestry. It does, however, help us to understand where we are coming from and the impact that our own personality will make upon vocation.

I have often interviewed couples and asked them to tell me why they were exploring their vocation. It was a helpful question in order to find out whether one or other of them was making the running and the other a reluctant follower, or whether the sense of vocation was equally owned by both. Usually it was owned by both, but they would often use very different vocabulary to describe their sense of being called. It was a very useful way to begin to explore their different personalities and how they integrated their different personalities within their marriage.

The Myers-Briggs indicators can help you to understand how personality differences might impact upon an understanding of vocation.

Reflect . . .

Whether or not you are familiar with your Myers-Briggs indicators, reflect on the above and ask yourself how your own personality affects how you feel about vocation. How do you experience your own sense of vocation?

Can you think of examples when you interviewed someone with a very different personality and experienced difficulties in relating to what was shared?

Generational issues

'Generation Xile'

The first biblical character to have what could be called a 'generational understanding' of his vocation appears to have been Isaiah.[14] In order to help us to understand better the context of his vocation, he spells out to us in Isaiah 6 the exact year of his calling, the year that King Uzziah died (which was 740 BC). His calling was shaped by what was going on within the Kingdom of Judah and the surrounding nations. He was aware of the growing strength and power of the Assyrians and their threat to Judah, and these factors shaped and informed his understanding of himself, his society and his calling. As a man of unclean lips living among a people of unclean lips, Isaiah could not separate himself from his own culture and what was going on within his culture at the time of his calling – he was responding to the needs of his generation. Isaiah is a contemporary of those other 'Generation Uzziah' prophets, Hosea and Jeremiah.

Isaiah also introduces us to the concept of three generational perspectives: the early part of the book of Isaiah is pre-Exile and the writing reflects the perspectives of God at work within Judah and Israel's history at that time; the end of the book of Isaiah is about 'Generation Return', those looking beyond the Exile, with optimism, to the rebuilding of Jerusalem; but there is also 'Generation Xile', the writings in the book of Isaiah that reflect the experiences and feelings of the Babylonian Exile.

While key historical events will shape generational understanding and give a sense of collective optimism or pessimism, we also find that generations are shaped in reaction to some of the values of the previous generation. Generation Xile were aware that they were being punished for the sins of their fathers – the behaviour of Israel that led to God bringing the Exile upon them. This, in itself, is likely to have shaped their collective attitudes and behaviour.

But, as well as a response to historical events and a reaction against the previous generation, 'Generation Xile' also represents a very different world view from that which had gone before. 'Generation Uzziah' made sense of what it meant to be God's chosen people facing the threat of exile, and 'Generation Return' developed their understanding within the optimism of the return, but 'Generation Xile' needed to make sense of being God's chosen people within the context of no longer living in the Promised Land. There is a paradigm in their thinking; their 'chosen-ness' needed to be understood in a new way. During the Exile, Isaiah developed an understanding of being chosen for task and responsibility, and of suffering on behalf of the nations, rather than of being chosen for privilege. The understanding of Israel as having a missionary purpose was developed within this paradigm. 'Generation Xile' needed to make sense of Israel's ongoing suffering. The understanding of Israel as the Suffering Servant came out of this view. Israel needed to suffer on behalf of the nations. Israel needed to suffer in order that the nations could be brought back to God.

A post-modern perspective

Isaiah introduces us to the idea that our vocation is shaped by the events and circumstances influencing our generation, he neatly offers us three different generational perspectives and he also shows us that there is not always a smooth transition or evolution from one generational perspective to another; sometimes what is going on within the world causes a paradigm shift and a very different world view evolves. We are living in a similar situation at this stage in our history. In our case the paradigm is post-modernism; those born since 1965 are the first generation to have been significantly shaped by post-modernity, rather than by modernity.

Paula Harris[15] helps us to understand post-modernity by quoting Jean-Francis Lyotard who, in his book *The Postmodern Condition* published in 1979, defined post-modernism as 'incredulity towards metanarratives':

> metanarratives being understood as universal guiding principles, systems of thought, grand stories that control, contain and interpret reality. It's easy enough to recognize a metanarrative – they are defended by force, perpetuate violence and are instruments of power. They ignore and obscure other local narratives, other versions of the truth. So post-modernity's incredulity functions to undermine and critique the 'grand story' theory of reality that props up false power structure. In other words, by asking questions, the post-modern opens up multiple stories. Post-modernity undermines metanarratives by exploring and listening to local narratives, other voices that have been marginalized or other understandings of reality.

But surely as Christians we are meant to believe in a metanarrative? Don't we believe that there is an absolute truth? Lyotard further writes: 'Post-modernism doesn't so much reject the concept of absolute objective truth but rather has grave doubts about the capacity of human reason to grasp that truth.'[16]

Post-modernism can be deeply threatening to Christians who have been brought up with a modernist understanding of their faith, and I have been to conferences that have pleaded for the clocks to be put back and modernist Christian values to again become the norm. Personally I find that it is reassuring to realize that this is not a new debate within the Church. At the end of the second century some theologians struggled with the fact that there were four different Gospels, giving four different narratives. The 'modernists' wanted only one Gospel to appear within the Canon of Scripture, and they wanted to create a master-narrative: Marcion suggested the exclusive use of Luke's Gospel and Tatian a rewritten, integrated

Gospel from the existing four. The 'post-modernists', championed by Irenaeus, Bishop of Lyons, won the day and four different Gospel accounts prevailed.[17]

A helpful understanding of generational issues that has evolved in recent years classifies those born before 1945 as 'boosters', influenced particularly by the Depression and the Second World War; those born between 1945 and 1964 as 'boomers', influenced particularly by the post-war boom and the Vietnam War and the reaction against it; and those born between 1965 and 1985 as 'Generation X', influenced particularly by post-modernism and events such as the threat of the Cold War and the damage to the ozone layer.

Although the analysis comes from a Western perspective, the impact of globalization suggests that the understanding that flows from it is valid to a greater or lesser extent in many parts of Africa, Asia and South America. I will attempt a brief description of these three generations, but for a fuller understanding I would recommend:

- 'Reflections on Attrition in Career Missionaries: a generational perspective into the future' by Kath Donovan and Ruth Myors, writing in *Too Valuable to Lose*, edited by William D. Taylor (William Carey Library, 1997) – this particularly explores issues to do with missionary attrition and selection;
- *Postmission: World mission by a post-modern generation*, edited by Richard Tiplady (Paternoster Press, 2002) – this gives a very full overview of Generation X and post-modernism; and
- *Honourably Wounded*, by Marjorie Foyle (Monarch, 2001) – Chapter 1 presents a brief and excellent overview of the characteristics of Generation X.

The formative experiences of the boosters, those born before 1945, mean that they have a great sense of duty, loyalty and perseverance and are sacrificial, hard-working generalists with a tremendous respect for strong leadership and institutional authority. Vulnerability and personal needs are not discussed and conflict is best suppressed and avoided. As Christians, there is likely to be a well-disciplined spiritual life, a deep, almost mystical, sense of God's calling and a lifelong commitment to one denomination or one mission agency.

In contrast the boomers, born between 1945 and 1965, take for granted the material prosperity that was the result of the hard work of the previous generation. The Vietnam War, and other world issues, led them to question and challenge authority and become idealistic, with a great sense of personal responsibility for their own choices and a respect and tolerance for others to make their own lifestyle choices. As they have worked through a time of great technological, and other, change they have become effective at managing change. Their respect and loyalty is for relationships and family, rather than institutions. As Christians they will want to find the best way, at any particular point in time, to use their God-given gifts for the good of the Kingdom.

Generation X, those born between 1965 and 1985, have been described as 'the harbingers of our very uncertain future' and 'the most indulged materially and the least nurtured of all generations'. They can be pessimistic because of the vulnerability of the planet and they are very aware of their own vulnerability. Many are products of fragmented families and victims of different forms of abuse. Often one of the reasons for family fragmentation has been the excessive hours put into work or duty, rather than family, by their parents (who are usually 'boosters'). Because of this vulnerability they are sensitive and have a longing for deep, lasting relationships and for belonging to teams. Mobile phones, email accounts and membership of a social networking group are icons of the instant communication that they will expect, wherever they are.

Post-modernism means an affirmation of the individual's narrative, rather than an acceptance of the 'metanarrative'; this has given Generation X a tolerance to different people's views, and a desire to be whole people affirming all of their life and not just work. None will have expectations of being in the same job for life, many will have experienced times of unemployment and most will change professions several times in their early career. Many will have become Christians as a result of experiencing God's grace within traumatic circumstances in their lives, and there is a hunger for spiritual things and experience rather than knowledge. Commitment will be shown to God and to a peer group, but not to a particular Church, denomination or mission agency; respect will need to be gained. They are unlikely to use the traditional language of vocation, and more likely to talk about how their own needs will be met.

Post-Christendom

Those born and brought up during the period of the Babylonian Exile were similarly the first Hebrew generation, since before the Exodus, who needed to try to make sense of living out their faith as a minority within a pluralistic society. They are closely paralleled by the first generation to be born and brought up without the assumptions of Christendom. The Christians who are Generation X are not only post-modern but also post-Christendom.

I cannot attempt to do justice to the issue of post-Christendom here, and for a fuller understanding I recommend Stuart Murray's book *Post-Christendom*,[18] so what follows is rather simplistic.

Since the time of Constantine, the empire – and more recently the nation state – has been assumed to be Christian. Those living within Christendom were exposed to the claims of Christianity, and shaped by a society, culture and educational systems that were meant to be built upon Christian assumptions. Christendom equated empire or nation with Church; those who belonged to the empire or nation were assumed to belong to the Church.

With this assumption there was no understanding of a need for mission. Mission was what happened in overseas countries outside Christendom, until they, too, became Christian and mission was no longer needed. Occasionally mission was what happened within 'mission churches', for the un-churched in the growing urban areas during the nineteenth century, but mission continued to be seen as separate from the mainline tasks of the Church. The vocational task of Christians within Christendom was primarily maintaining the Church, rather than sharing the faith among those who had not heard it.

Before Constantine became a Christian, the pre-Christendom Church was a persecuted minority, often made up of the marginal-ized, and functioning at the edges of society. The move from the margins to a position of influence within Christendom allowed much that was good to happen within society, but it also dulled much of the prophetic voice of the Church, so that now it is often seen not as an instrument of positive change but as a force of conservatism committed to retaining the status quo. In the pre-Christendom Church, the ministry of the Word would often involve discussion, with each member of the Church expected to share what his or her personal experience brought to the text. Christendom affirmed the sermon as a means of control, but such a didactic style of teaching does not sit comfortably with post-modernism.

Although the Church that is the remnant of Christendom is shrinking,[19] post-Christendom has brought about many new expressions of Church, both within and outside the traditional denominations. These post-Christendom churches will have an emphasis on mission and on different styles of worship and learning and different ways of being Church. Although some of their members will have migrated from existing churches, others will be un-churched and have come from a non-Christian background.

Post-denominational

Our denominations are a product of Christendom. The political tensions, and language differences, within the Holy Roman Empire, between the Latin-speaking West and the Greek-speaking East led to the split between the Roman Catholic Church and the Orthodox Churches. The development of nation states, combined with the Reformation, meant that Christendom splintered further, with the established church being Anglican, Lutheran or Presbyterian in different parts of northern Europe. The other denominations developed largely either as splinter movements from these denominations or as reactions to them.

It is not surprising that in some parts of the world outside Christendom, where Christians are in a minority, denominations have been viewed as a hangover from European culture, and there is a 'post-denominational' Church in China and a non-denominational Church in Nepal. The 'United Churches' of the Indian subcontinent came into being after independence because denominational differences within the Church were seen as a barrier to mission.

Generation X, as post-modern and post-Christendom people, tend to have little commitment to a particular denomination. They are relational and experiential people, who will choose their church because of the people or because of the experience, rather than for doctrinal reasons. As my name suggests, my own family roots are within Scotland, that part of Christendom that was Presbyterian, and I was brought up as a Presbyterian in England but am now an Anglican. Until writing this I had always assumed that my decision to become an Anglican was a doctrinal one. I am now left wondering whether it was an acceptance that I belonged to a different part of Christendom (England rather than Scotland) – experiential because of the style of worship or relational because of the people I knew. In reality there are probably aspects of each of these within my spiritual journey.

I believe that we live within a very exciting and challenging era of Christian history. Just as the Exile was an important time of reflection and re-evaluation for the Hebrew people, leading to a far deeper understanding of God's nature and purposes, so does the emergence of our own 'Generation Xile' offer exciting, creative opportunities. Christ came to redeem all people of all cultures and all nations and he is just as relevant for our post-modern, post-Christendom, post-denominational era as he was for previous eras. Despite the fact that many traditional ministries are struggling to recruit those who are aged under 40, there are many young people, often including those who have come originally from non-Christian backgrounds, who feel called by God to serve in this way. The fact that we use terms such as 'post-modern', 'post-Christendom' and 'post-denominational' also reminds us that we are still in a period of transition. When transition is complete then a new era should have its own name, rather than being classified as 'post-the previous era'.

Another issue related to the testing of vocation is that if the understanding of mission or ministry has been developed by boosters and if the selection processes are mainly in the hands of boosters or boomers, then it can be very easy to identify the generational differences as weaknesses and failures of Generation X, and not take their calling seriously. Yet there are many young people involved in church plants, youth ministry and new expressions of Church; these are not the types of vocation that you will find out about at most traditional vocational events.

The understanding that I have gained over the years is that Generation X have much to offer the Christian mission and the ministry.

- Although I have found myself interviewing far more people who have experienced fragmentation and trauma within their families or their own lives, this has often resulted in a really deep and personal testimony to God's grace within their life.
- Similarly, those who have come to a living faith from outside the Church tend to have far more of a heart for mission than those brought up within the Church; they also have a story to share of their own conversion.
- There is a changing attitude to baptism; many who were baptized as children, based upon a decision made by their parents, will want to make their own decision to be baptized. More Christian parents will want to have a service of thanksgiving for their new babies and leave them to make their own mind up about being baptized when they are old enough to make their own personal decision.
- Generation X are far more open about their vulnerability and hurts. Previous generations are more likely to have suppressed such vulnerabilities and not addressed them, so that either they are still there waiting to surface or they are stopping people from functioning as effectively as they might.
- As a consequence of this, Generation X are more likely to have dealt with problems and be aware of the pastoral support that they need in order to function effectively, rather than being in a state of denial about the need for such support.
- For Generation X, there can be self-doubt, and the need for affirmation.
- Generation X desire truth and authenticity and prefer that people 'tell it as it is'. Their perception of the lack of these qualities has often led them to be cynical and sceptical.
- Generation X are more likely to be direct, open and honest and to be able to tackle conflict situations.
- Generation X want to develop their own identity, will affirm diversity and are not afraid of those who have different views from their own. Other faiths and world views are neither dismissed as irrelevant nor absorbed as being variations of the same story, but are engaged with constructively.
- Generation X are team workers and believe that leaders need to prove their ability to lead rather than be accepted without question as authority figures.

- Generation X tend to be flexible and adaptable.
- Generation X are holistic people who seek a balanced life, rather than putting duty and career first at the possible expense of family and health.
- Being holistic people means holding together faith with other aspects of life and avoiding the temptation to keep different parts of life within different boxes.
- To be a post-Christendom Christian means that you are more likely to be living out your faith among non-Christians, to have worked it out for yourself and to have a commitment to a counter-cultural world view, compared with your contemporaries.
- Generation X believe in learning through experience and that gaining short-term experience will be a way of beginning to test vocation.
- Generation X's post-denominationalism stems from a commitment to Christ, rather than to human institutions.
- We might expect to see a hesitancy from those in their 20s and 30s to commit themselves for the next 30 or 40 years to a ministry that is perceived as maintaining a diminishing or dying expression of Church.
- Although there is not loyalty to institutions, denominations and mission agencies, and respect needs to be earned, there can still be great loyalty when such respect has been gained and a relationship has been developed.

Taking Generation X seriously may well mean re-evaluating the outworking of mission or ministry within the Church or organization, in order to hear what God is saying. It may also mean that selection processes need to be reviewed.

- An obvious first step with any 'cross-cultural' selection is to include people from that culture as interviewers within the selection process!
- It is very difficult for those without specific professional training to be able to make decisions about deeply traumatic and painful issues, and it may be helpful at times to involve a psychiatrist, or other professional, within the selection processes.
- We can expect a greater openness to be expressed about vulnerability and recognition of the pastoral and spiritual support that will be required. If we are conditioned to see such an

understanding of vulnerability as a weakness, then we will need to re-evaluate our own understanding.

- We cannot expect to hear vocation described in neat formulae, but we can expect to hear something that is authentically making sense to the person from his or her own experience.
- We can expect to hear other world views being taken more seriously than in the past, and for people to show a greater capacity to engage – with curiosity, understanding and empathy – with these world views.
- Because we live within a time of transition between Christendom and post-Christendom vocational opportunities, we may easily find that those who are nudged by God are actually trying the wrong door. We may need to be more discerning about what people are actually being called to.
- Those testing their vocation with a mission agency will usually be making explorations with a number of agencies before deciding which is the best match for them.
- There will be higher expectations of definite information about the role and about terms and conditions of service.
- We will expect to have to answer more questions about what happens and why and about the thinking, ethos and strategy that underlie our answers.

Generation Y

More recent social commentators refer to those born towards the end of the twentieth century as Generation Y and those born in the twenty-first century as Generation Z. Within these definitions there is debate as to when Generation X ceased and Generation Y began. Early comments on Generation Y spoke of the optimism experienced in moving into the new millennium and being shaped by the communication revolution of universal internet access; more recent commentators have referred to life post-9/11 and the war against terror. An internet search of 'Generation Y' or 'Generation Z' will show more recent articles and books describing these generations. I don't yet feel that I have had enough experience of interviewing Generation Y and, obviously, I have had no experience of interviewing Generation Z to be able to integrate my own experiences with what has been written in the way that I can with the three generations described above.

As mentioned, each generation will define itself to some extent in reaction against the previous generation as well as in response to world events, and we can expect to find this in Generations Y and Z. What made Generation X so different from the previous generations was the paradigm shifts of post-modernity and post-Christendom. I don't believe that we will experience any such paradigms with Generations Y and Z, but I would encourage the reader to relate what is written to their own experiences of interviewing those born since the mid 1980s and try to make sense of it in the light of what I have said above.

Personality and the vocabulary of vocation

I asked in the first chapter, 'What influences the vocabulary people use to describe their sense of call?' I would suggest that both their personality and their generational perspective will be very important influences. Three other influences will be:

- the teaching of their church;
- role models that they have come across; and
- books that they have read.

It is easy to find examples of a tension between the understanding of vocation that has been picked up from church teaching, books and role models compared with what is real for people because of their personality.

Often, because of the words that people are familiar with, there can be an assumption that vocation should be expressed with particular words or formulae, even though such words or formulae do not do justice to what they have personally experienced or to what they really think or feel.

Reflect . . .

What tensions, if any, exist between the teaching on vocation that you have experienced and what is 'real' for you as a consequence of your personality or generational perspective? How do you cope with any such tension?

Our role in exploring vocation will include exploring any such tension, to try to get to what is really motivating the candidate. Personally, I don't think it is appropriate to judge candidates for using the vocabulary that they have been brought up with, but it is useful to help them explore this tension and discover what is real for them.

Part 2
DEVELOPING A STRATEGY

4

Person specifications and vocation

Reflect . . .

Do you have a form of 'person specification' or list of 'competencies' for your ministry? If not, what are the reasons for not having them?

Person specifications

Traditionally, if you are trying to fill a particular post, you will draw up a job description, prioritizing the purpose of the post and its key responsibilities, and then use this to draw up a person specification. With many Christian vocations, however, the type of roles that are being filled cannot be readily pigeon-holed into a job description, so it can be difficult to see how to draw up such a person specification. Some organizations do list the specific competencies that are required for the vocation, but even this is not straightforward for some vocations.

Even if it is not possible to draw up a detailed person specification or list of competencies, I would like to suggest a five-stage process to try to give some shape to a person specification.

1 Why do we have this ministry?

It's helpful to go right back to basics and ask why you actually want someone in the position that you are trying to fill; so for example, ask yourself 'Why do we want clergy?' or 'Why do we send mission partners?' You might expect the answers to be obvious, but they can often reflect the changes that have taken place within the ministry over recent years.

Clergy are now seen as those who can enable the laity, rather than as those who do everything for the laity; increasingly they are seen as those who should be involved in, and nurturing, the mission of the Church, rather than just supporting its ministry. By looking at these expectations of a particular ministry, some qualities should become apparent.

Mission partners from the UK need to be a channel for informing and challenging the British churches with insights from overseas churches; if they are expected to be able to share their faith within a culture dominated by another world view then they need to have a faith, have experience of sharing their faith and be able to relate their faith to a different world view, and so on.

2 What makes a good or bad . . . ?

Everyone can think of people involved in different ministries who shine out as good examples, and those who are a disaster and should never have been selected. If you can define the reasons for this then you can add to the list qualities that are wanted, and those that should be avoided. Often such answers will focus particularly around people skills.

3 What is the ethos of the organization?

If your organization has an ethos statement or a set of core values, then this again adds to the attributes that can be listed.

Under this heading it will be important to consider whether there is a policy on sexuality and guidelines with reference to any specific categories of people (but see p. 73). It is far better to develop policy and guidelines objectively, rather than on the hoof when someone is part way through your selection process. You might consider developing your core values outline at an 'away day' where different groups can work on different aspects before coming together to produce a statement.

4 What are the role-specific attributes?

Having said that vocation cannot be easily defined within a job description and person specification, there may be attributes that can be identified for specific roles within that form of ministry. If the role has responsibilities for leading worship, teaching and preaching, pastoral care, enabling others or administration, then these attributes can be defined.

5 What are the location-specific attributes?

If the vocation is to be lived out within a specific location, there might be a number of attributes that can be identified for that specific location. It is possible to draw up pro formas to give an idea of the importance of different attributes for different locations.

From these five exercises, it is possible to identify many of the qualities and attitudes that are generally required within the ministry in question. Looking at this list you will probably notice some factors or personality traits that you definitely don't want; conversely, this will lead to you putting certain attributes on your essential list. You will also notice that there are some qualities that are 'teachable'; these can be put down as desirable. In looking at what might be teachable, you might identify factors that will inhibit learning, in which case other attributes may be added to the essential list.

By dividing these attributes into essential and desirable, you can begin to draw up a person specification. The first three exercises provide a generic person specification; you can then use the last two exercises to add subsections relating to specific types of ministry or specific locations.

A sense of vocation

Having drawn up such a profile, you may easily find that it could be filled by any mature Christian with certain relevant professional or people skills. But we are talking of Christian vocation, not Christian jobs, and so the first and most important part of the person specification will be a sense of vocation, or the 'God factor'.

The God factor

The qualities mentioned above are all ones that might be readily defined and reasonably easy to quantify. The exploration of the sense of vocation will be harder to define. Chapter 1 explores different understandings of vocation, Chapter 2 explores how vocation is something that grows, and Chapter 3 shows how understandings of vocation can be influenced by personality and generational issues. These understandings will all help to define the task.

Reflect . . .

In the light of what you have read in the previous three chapters, and your own experience, list what issues you might wish to consider in exploring vocation.

The exploration of vocation might include the following:

- how Christian vocation has been understood and outworked in the past;
- the sense of distinct purpose, and the way in which life would not feel complete if certain visions are not fulfilled;
- the first discovery of the seed of vocation, and its nurture and growth over a period of time;
- the identification of, use and growth of talents, and the awareness of talents that are still being developed;
- the sense of having a vocation identified, nurtured and affirmed by part of the wider Body of Christ;
- an awareness of motivation and a self-awareness of some of the complexities of motivation;
- an exploration of the humanity, as well as the faith and sense of task and whether vocation is being built upon firm foundations or is a compensation for vulnerabilities;
- the interaction of faith upon humanity and vocation and whether there are appropriate boundaries between the three;
- an exploration of the emotional ups and downs of life and where God has been within these, and an awareness of whether decisions have been made during times of consolation or desolation;
- an awareness of God taking away barriers of unworthiness or inadequacy, perhaps an 'Isaiah 6' experience of no longer feeling unclean or too sinful;
- the self-understanding of gifts and characteristics, and how these do, or don't, flow through humanity, faith and vocation;
- an awareness of relationships and the dynamics involved within relationships, and of the impact that the vocation is likely to make upon relationships within the congregation;

- an honest understanding of expectations, and previous experience of needing to modify expectations and to cope with difference and change;
- an awareness of training needs and an openness to vocational training and to being stretched and changed through living outside familiar comfort zones;
- a realistic understanding of the impact of a particular vocation upon other members of the family and the sacrifices that might be demanded of them and, with certain ministries, a jointly owned sense of vocation;
- the capacity to continue to learn and grow and to reach a fuller potential in Christ;
- a sense of obedience to God's leading in the past, as well as in the present;
- a sense of vocation that seems to be true to personality, rather than inherited from other people's understanding of vocation;
- a sense of God's leading that is described in words that are real to that person, and their experience of God at work within their lives, rather than neat spiritual clichés; and
- an appropriate balance between loyalty to a vision, appropriate use of God-given skills and awareness of vulnerability.

But what do we mean by saying a sense of obedience to God's leading? For me, the bottom line is that when the going gets tough, as it is likely to do at some point within any Christian vocation, the accepted candidate will have a deep assurance of being where God wants. For this to happen the candidate will need to be able to articulate that sense of God's leading in a way that makes personal sense. But the candidate will also need to know that others have affirmed that sense of leading within his or her life. For the latter to have occurred the candidate's sense of leading will need to have been articulated in such a way that others can understand it, question it and affirm it.

The sense of God's leading may be expressed in various ways; ultimately, there is a sense of God communicating with the person and, although this is a personal and intimate experience, it is important for this to be articulated. In Chapter 2 of *On Call*, I have explored some of the ways in which some of the biblical characters appear to hear God speak to them and how these might not vary so much from the experiences of those who are aware of God speaking to them today. For Peter, being told in triplicate to 'kill and eat' (Acts 10) follows the same pattern as his three-fold denial (John 18) and his three-fold commissioning at the lakeside (John 21), and surely makes him realize that his vision is from the Lord. We, too, can expect to find God speaking to us now in ways familiar to us from how he has spoken to us in the past.

You may also want to explore how a person has responded to the sense of God's leading. Chapter 3 of *On Call* explores the biblical wrestling with God: the feelings of unfairness – questioning why Jacob was chosen rather than Esau (Genesis 27); unworthiness – Isaiah's vision in the temple (Isaiah 6); and self-doubt (Jeremiah 1). Again these can be very real responses in developing understanding of a call. There will often be a real sense of challenge to the vocation, which might be seen to be rooted in a lack of self-esteem or the outworking of spiritual forces.

Building up the picture

It is all very well to list the factors that might contribute to an understanding of vocation, but how do we explore this? It is helpful to examine the backdrop of how candidates have got to where they are now: why they have begun this particular journey at this stage in their life? To make sense of their answers you will want to discuss what has been going on in their lives to shape their self-understanding and their understanding of what is happening now.

To do this effectively, you will need to understand what influences have shaped them and led them to make decisions in the past, to get a picture of their self-worth and how this has been shaped, how they develop and sustain relationships, and their coping strategies. Within all of this you will need to try to understand how their faith has developed, how it has been sustained and how it has been challenged.

This backdrop can be built up by investigating the following.

- The family that they were born into; what their parents did; what siblings they had, and their chronological position within the family; the family dynamics; what moves or traumas were faced by the family and the age and stage of schooling at the time; how they got on at school and whether they lived in the shadow of some of their siblings – from all of this you can get a picture of security and relationships that were formulating the early years, and this will help you to understand how candidates have reached their current sense of self-worth and their confidence in making and developing relationships.

- How professional choices were made; how these compared with the professional choices made by other members of the family; how their professional choices have been accepted and affirmed by others within the family – this will begin to give you insights into how decisions have been made, and whether members of the family support, oppose or are indifferent to the vocation.
- How faith became real and personal – for candidates from a Christian family, it will usually have been when they were away from family influences that they will know that their faith was theirs, and not just a common trait; how their faith is different from that of other members of the family, and how such differences are coped with; what difference faith has made to lifestyle, and how others have perceived the difference that their faith has made to them.
- How faith has been challenged by study, the lifestyle of friends or their jobs; how faith has been challenged by other Christians, different styles of worship, different faiths and world views; how faith has been nurtured and how it has coped with crisis, rebellion and dry times.

For more on how to explore these issues, see Chapters 13 and 14. With this understanding of how their humanity and faith have been shaped, and how they have impinged upon each other, you can feel confident to begin to make sense of what a candidate is saying about his or her calling to a Christian vocation.

5

A selection strategy

Purpose of the selection process

> *Reflect . . .*
>
> What are you trying to achieve through your selection processes?

Asking what the purpose of your selection process is may sound an obvious question, but my own understanding of what can be achieved through selection processes developed over time and has been informed by helping different groups to explore this question. Although I offer some answers below, I would suggest you explore this question before reading what follows.

My own answer to this question is that I want to help the candidate to reach his or her full potential in Christ, and in order to do this it needs to be established if the candidate's vocation truly lies in the agency and in the position that I am selecting for. If your organization's purpose is similar, you will need to do the following.

1 Test vocation to church or agency

The first task is to find out whether candidates have a vocation to serve with your agency – whether:

- they have a vocation to the type of ministry that you offer;
- they have the skills and attributes that you are seeking;
- they have an understanding of your church or organization, and the empathy with your ethos, vision and values to be able to work out their vocation with you;
- they will be able to blossom and grow through a ministry with you;
- you and they feel that God has called them to such a ministry with you.

2 Determine parameters that might have an impact on suitable locations and settings to work out that vocation

There will also be parameters that will influence where that ministry can best be carried out. Some locations could be counterproductive whereas others could enable the candidate to blossom and grow. You will want to know how best to use candidates for the Kingdom. You shouldn't expect that their vocation will necessarily always be within the same location, so you will need to look at the factors that might determine locations after training and at subsequent points within their ministry.

3 Determine learning needs

You don't want to provide people with training that they have already had, or with training that would be inappropriate for them. This means you need to establish the best learning programme for their own personal development for the possible ministry that they will go to. You will need to explore what they have done and what the gaps are, so that a learning programme can be drawn up with them.

4 Determine pastoral support

Having trained and located the candidate, you will need to make sure that appropriate pastoral support is in place to allow him or her to function and grow. You'll therefore need to be aware of individual pastoral needs.

5 Determine spiritual support

Similarly, to help candidates to grow and develop as Christians it will be important for you to be aware of their spiritual needs.

6 Affirm as a Christian, loved, valued and called to some purpose by God

Whether or not a person is selected by you, you will want that person to have found that going through your processes has been as positive an experience as possible, and that even if this particular door of opportunity has closed, the process will have helped the person to understand why this is so and to have a better understanding of how and where he or she may be able to fulfil the vocation.

Our relationship with God is a very intimate relationship. If we have felt that God was saying something to us but the wider Body disagrees with this conclusion, it can raise questions about the validity of what we have understood that God has said to us in the past and our confidence in how we might be able to hear him speak to us in the future. Ultimately, it can raise questions about the assumptions at the centre of our faith.

The selection strategy window

My starting point in developing a selection strategy window is the Johari model, developed by American psychologists Joseph Luft and Harry Ingham in the 1950s while they were researching group dynamics. This model forms a grid by looking at what a person knows about himself or herself and what others know about the person. Within any encounter between two people there are four distinct window-panes of information formed by the intersection of what one person knows and does not know about himself or herself and what the other person knows and does not know. These intersections can be classified as: open, blind, hidden, and unknown or potential.

Although the Johari model is an excellent tool for the purposes for which it was developed, it's necessary to modify it slightly when using it to test vocation. For selection purposes it isn't just a matter of the selectors knowing or not knowing something about a candidate, but there is a wide continuum of possibilities in between, such as:

- I don't know, but I am pretty sure.
- I don't know, but it has been hinted at.
- I don't know, but it is a possibility.
- I don't know, but I would want to find it out about anyone.
- I don't think or feel it is likely, but I suppose I had better check it out.
- I don't know, and wouldn't even dream of assuming such a thing.

In order to make a workable tool these options can be reduced to three categories.

1 The selectors know: we have evidence to come to this conclusion.

2 The selectors think: we don't know conclusively, but what we have found out, or heard from others, suggests that this is the case.
3 The selectors don't know: we don't have enough information even to begin to make a judgement.

These three categories (see pp. 48–9) can then be used to form the basis of a selection strategy window (see p. 50). From this model I would suggest the following:

1 Selection processes should be based upon **evidence**, which is information that we have in the **selectors know** row, rather than **intuition**, which belongs in the **selectors think** row. We can function in two different ways, and the style that we favour is likely to be due to our personality. Some people will naturally consider all of the available evidence and come to what they regard as a reasoned conclusion based upon this evidence. Others will depend more upon their feelings and intuitively come to a conclusion. Of course there is an overlap. What might appear to be a highly intuitive decision might be feelings that come as the result of the available evidence. A decision made on evidence might be the result of intuitively deciding that some evidence should carry more weight than other evidence.

   Having said that, I feel that intuition is an important part of the selection process. If you are an intuitive person, you may have a feeling that you particularly need to explore a certain area or issue or that the way into a certain issue is to ask a particular question. Intuition is what helps you decide what needs exploring; you can then explore the issue and seek the evidence on which to make a decision. You must, of course, be prepared for your intuition to have been wrong; you must not prejudge the evidence but must keep an open mind.

2 Selectors might feel confident in making decisions with information that they know but that the candidate doesn't know, but they can't then be transparent with the candidate. If you wish to minimize the pastoral and spiritual damage to those whom you do not accept and if you wish to engage openly and honestly with their learning needs, pastoral and spiritual support and location parameters, you need to get as much information as possible out of the other five domains into the **open** domain, where it is known to the candidate as well as the selectors.

Selection strategy window

	The candidate knows	The candidate does not know
The selectors know	*Open* Evidence known to the candidate and the selectors; for example: factual information from the CV or application forms and factual information shared in previous interviews	*Blind* Behaviour, feelings and motivation known to others and not to the candidate. Often this domain will be empty but it might include, for example: information about relationships or sensitivities that the selectors feel they have confirmed from different sources
The selectors think	*Suspected assumptions* Assumptions about the candidate that the candidate is aware of which the selectors have made or heard from other people and think might be true; for example: assumptions based upon facts that the candidate has shared with other interviewers	*Unsuspected assumptions* Assumptions about the candidate that the candidate is not aware of, which the selectors have made or heard from other people and think might be true; for example: assumptions from reading between the lines of what has been shared with other interviewers and some confidential comments in references
The selectors don't know	*Hidden* The candidate's thoughts, beliefs, feelings, needs, wants, values etc, known to the candidate but not to the selectors; for example: things that the candidate knows about himself or herself but has not shared with anyone else	*Unknown/potential* The possibilities and potential of the candidate that are not known to the candidate or the selectors; for example: how the candidate will cope with situations that he or she has not yet encountered

3 Within your processes, you need to find ways to move assumptions from the **selectors think** row into knowledge in the **selectors know** row. This might mean that something you

thought was true is proved not to be a true assumption; either way it now belongs in the **selectors know** row and the **open** domain.

4 If you ask a question that leads, for example, to your hearing about a time when the candidate dealt satisfactory with particular stressful events, learnt about himself or herself and grew, then you need to be careful what information you put into which domain. You don't actually know that currently and in the future the candidate can cope well with stress. Although the facts and narrative of that particular episode do belong in the **open** domain, it is still only an assumption that the candidate can actually cope well with stress, on the basis of an exploration of just one episode, and therefore it belongs in the **selectors think** row. Further exploration of other potentially stressful events will be needed before the candidate's ability, or otherwise, to cope with stress can be moved into the **open** domain.

5 Information that comes from references, home churches, group activities and so on is generally assumptions that belong in the **selectors think** row rather than the **selectors know** row. You would then need to explore what this information is saying and reach conclusions as to what should end up in the **selectors know** row. To do this, it is no good obtaining and using this information after the final interviews have taken place.

   Mention is made later of personality and ability testing. Those designing such tests might argue that the results are knowledge rather than assumptions. But given that the results are usually based upon statistical likelihood, it can also be argued that they are assumptions rather than knowledge. You probably should not justify non-selection purely upon the basis of such tests. If you do use them, do so to help you determine the assumptions that need to be explored further in order to obtain evidence within the **open** domain.

6 When you have assumptions, from your own intuition, references or other sources, you need to explore the issues in the **candidate knows** column, to move information from **selectors think** row to the **selectors know** row. If the issue is also in the **candidate does not know** column, then for the sake of transparency you need to find ways to move it into the **candidate knows** column and the **open** domain.

7 The issues in the **unknown or potential** domain can best be explored within the **hidden** domain (the candidate's thoughts, feelings, values etc), but the **selectors think** row might give you some clues. You need to try and get as much of this information as possible into the **open** domain.

8 It may be that there is no available evidence to help you, or the candidate, to explore a particular issue in the **unknown or potential** domain, and you will need to encourage the candidate to gain further experience before an adequate exploration of the issue that provides evidence is possible.

9 It is possible that our explorations will move something from the **unknown or potential** domain to the **hidden** domain and make the candidate decide not to pursue the application any further. In that case you don't need to know what it was about nor do you need to move the issue in to the **open** domain.

Real life . . .

A couple did not have enough experience for their ability to cope with extreme and sustained cross-cultural living to be assessed. It was suggested that they gain some experience and then come back for further interview. They gained some experience, and then decided themselves not to take their enquiry any further.

---

10 Some selection processes appear to function with all the selectors using their own selection window, and decisions will then be determined, to a large extent, by the dynamics between the different selectors. The reason for such a starting point may be that each interviewer wishes to 'come in fresh' and 'make his or her own decision about the candidate, rather than be influenced by previous interviews'. If you are careful to put only facts and narrative into the **selectors know** row, and keep assumptions and opinions in the **selectors think** row, then this shouldn't be an issue.

The fact that different selectors can look at the same narrative or facts from their different perspectives, and come up with different assumptions is helpful, as long as they then objectively seek the evidence that is needed to put the issue in to the **selectors know** row and the **open** domain.

The best way to get material into the **open** domain is to pool the facts and narrative in the candidate's file and make sure that this material is used by all of those involved in the selection process.

11 The selection process needs to have enough stages in it to allow proper exploration of material, such as references, that produces assumptions. It will be through further interviewing that these assumptions can be confirmed or proved wrong and conclusions added to the **open** domain.

12 Within the European Union, a candidate may ask to read the information that is held on file (for more on this see p. 76). If you hold narrative, factual material that is in the **open** domain combined with questions of what else you wish to explore, rather than assumptions that belong in other domains, you should have nothing to worry about if candidates read their files.

Chapter 13 explores interview techniques and considers how some of the above might be achieved.

Reflect . . .

Look at your own processes and see whether they allow these 12 aims to be achieved. If not, which ones might you engage with? How might you need to modify your process?

Intuitive processes

In Chapter 13, in exploring how to gain evidence to make selection decisions, I suggest that an exploration of times of change can produce much helpful material. Sometimes we meet with people who have had very little experience of such times of change. In particular, if you have a programme for those who are just leaving school and who have never lived away from the family home, it is very difficult to gain enough evidence to make selection decisions. In such cases a selection process will need to have a major focus upon intuitive processes in which the candidates are exposed to ideas, situations and role plays and their responses to these are explored.

As mentioned, it is not easy to explain to someone why you have turned them down for reasons based upon intuition, rather than evidence. If a major part of the selection is based upon the intuitive response of the selectors to exercises, it can be very helpful then to use an interview to explore further the responses and reactions and to assist the candidate to reflect upon these and bring the information and evidence into the **open** domain. Such discussions can then be the basis for giving a selection decision based upon evidence.

Who else is affected by the vocation?

With anyone pursuing a Christian vocation there is likely to be some impact upon their immediate and wider family. Pursuing a Christian vocation usually means making some sacrifices with regard to income, where you will live and your free time. It also means that people other than family will often have expectations of you and your availability. Meeting these expectations can easily clash with the expectations of family.

Many vocations require a physical move of location; perhaps initially for training before commencing the actual work. If the vocation is to be incarnationally out-worked in an area of need then the move will probably be to an area that offers poorer schools for children and to an area traditionally associated with a poorer quality of life. With the wider family, these will be issues to explore as part of the selection process. With the immediate family, there will be a need to explore how much they also feel called to these choices.

Most mission agencies that are involved in moving people from one country to another will clearly feel that the vocation needs to belong to both husband and wife and would be very wary of a call that was owned by only one half of a couple. In such a case husband and wife ought to come through the selection process as equals.

There are other vocations in which the spouse would not be expected necessarily to share, but that would nonetheless have a deep impact on him or her. Returning to the selection strategy window, the important issue will be that decisions are made that are based upon knowledge, rather than assumptions, of how the spouse feels about the vocation.

Another concern should be the impact upon children. By the time children begin school they will have made friends and will usually be reluctant to be uprooted and moved to another place. This is not in itself a reason not to go ahead because any family moving as the result of a job change would face this situation. It will, however, be important to explore whether the children have any social or educational needs that will not be met in the place where the vocation will be out-worked. With cross-cultural mission in a different country it has been suggested that it is not advisable to move children to another country, for first-time service, once they have reached puberty; both puberty and the move to another country provide enough changes to cope with on their own.

As children begin to approach puberty it is probably worth trying to find some more objective ways to explore their expectations, aspirations and anxieties. However, in the same way that decisions should not be made just upon the assumptions of the parents about their children, it will be important that decisions are not made from assumptions about their children that are not understood or accepted by the parents. In all of this, it will be important to develop processes that move as much information as possible from the **selectors think** row into the **open** domain.

6

Selecting cross-culturally

Selecting from different cultures raises a lot of issues, and there's no magic formula that can be applied whenever you interview someone from a different culture. It's possible, however, to learn how to avoid mistakes that have been made in the past, and to become aware of your own limitations.

> **Reflect . . .**
>
> What challenges have you been aware of in selecting those from different cultures? How have you responded to these challenges?

Limited perspectives

In the late 1970s I taught physics and mathematics to teenagers at a girls' secondary school in a rural area of East Africa. Twenty-five years later, I found myself interviewing two different East African couples. In both cases one partner came from the area that I had taught in and would have been at secondary school at the time that I had been teaching in that area. Not only was I aware of some of the issues that they would have faced, but I was also aware of the traditional attitudes between their tribe and the tribe of their spouse. As I explored their vocation, I felt very aware of some of the relevant issues and the questions to ask. In particular there was much I could ask about the sensitivities involved in establishing a marriage between members of two tribes that traditionally had very little time and sympathy for each other.

As I wrote up my interview report I bathed, for a few moments, in that nice warm glow of how good an interviewer I was, and how my previous experiences meant that I knew the right questions to ask. It didn't last for long before I became conscious of how few parts of the world I have such deep knowledge and understanding of. Although I might expect to be able to get this depth of information from those who had lived in that part of East Africa and had been of a particular age at a particular time, I became deeply aware that I did not have the experience to explore issues so deeply for those who lived in other parts of East Africa, other parts of Africa and other parts of the world, other than the UK.

Interestingly, the selection of both of those couples felt very straightforward, the interview reports had the quality of information that we would generally expect from our processes, and a quick look at the other paperwork showed application forms and references that were similar in length and in depth of information to those found when UK people came through our process. Both couples came from Christian families and had been educated within education systems that were very similar to those found within the UK. Often when I have interviewed those who come originally from a different faith background, or who have been brought up within a culture that is dominated by another faith understanding, it has been more difficult for me to make sense of their narrative and to understand the factors that were really involved as they made choices and applied their world view to their life.

Avoiding stereotypes

Interviewing those from other countries and different cultures informs us and helps us to build up a fuller picture for the future, but it can also build up unhelpful stereotypes. I have interviewed a few people who have converted from other faiths, but their attitude to their pre-Christian lives, and their ability to see God at work within their lives at that stage, was quite different. I have also interviewed two different couples from the same eastern European country and encouraged them both to reflect upon the Communist and post-Communist eras: I heard totally different conclusions from both parties in each couple.

It is useful to know enough about a country or culture to know what events or issues could have had an impact upon someone's life and faith. These issues can then become a backdrop to explore their decision-making and how they relate faith to life, but it is dangerous to make any assumptions about what the right answers should be.

The climate between different faith communities can vary widely. I read a lovely story of a Good Friday procession of faith in an Indian city; members of the other faith communities offered the Christians drinks and refreshments as they marched past their own places of worship. In many other parts of the world, including parts of the UK, a Christian procession might have been seen as highly provocative and could easily have produced insults and stones, rather than drinks and food! Attitudes between different faith communities vary not only from country to country, but also within countries.

To make sense of people's experiences it will be important to ask more questions to clarify the circumstances and what was happening and why, and it will be important to clarify that we have fully understood what we have heard and have not added two and two to get five.

Reflect . . .

What other cultures do you personally have experience or knowledge of? How has this experience helped you with selecting people from that culture? Has your previous knowledge ever created unhelpful stereotypes?

Cultural stereotypes in a global world

In 1968 and 1972, Gerard Hendrik Hofstede carried out a huge survey of 116,000 employees, from 72 countries, in one multinational company.[20] This helpful research, revised in 1994, quantified certain personality traits within different cultures. He explored five different measures:

1 power distance – the extent to which the less powerful members of organizations and institutions accept and expect power to be distributed unequally;
2 uncertainty avoidance – the extent to which a culture expects its members to feel comfortable in unstructured situations;

3 individualism versus collectivism – the degree to which people are supposed to look after themselves or remain integrated into groups;

4 masculinity versus femininity – the distribution of emotional roles between the sexes; and

5 long-term versus short-term – the extent to which members of a culture accept delayed gratification of their material, social and emotional needs.

Globalization means that much has changed since such research was conducted, and far more people are subject to influences from outside their own culture. If someone enquires of your organization from another country, then it will usually be as the result of information discovered on the internet. The very fact that someone from another country is in touch with you is, in itself, the result of globalization, and you must expect such an enquirer to have been influenced by many factors from outside their own culture and that such quantifiable research is therefore now of very limited value.

Clashes within cultures

Mention used to be made, in books about cross-cultural mission, about the clash between cultures. Increasingly, the emphasis now is upon the clash within cultures. How do people understand themselves as a product of their own culture, what other factors have influenced them from outside their culture, and how do they cope with the differences that they experience within their own culture and between their personal culture and the cultural norm? It is within this context that it can be helpful to have an awareness of cultural stereotypes, including the five measures listed above, so that deviation from such stereotypes can be observed and the reasons behind these explored.

Global people and third-culture children

Increasingly there are people who do not consider themselves as fitting neatly into any one culture. Schooling may have been in one country, tertiary education in another and work in yet another. For many, their families no longer live in the place where they spent their childhood and so there is no real sense of being rooted. For example, one such family, in discussing their sense of being global people rather than rooted anywhere, mentioned the different ethnic backgrounds of their children's godparents to make their point.

A specific subgroup of the global people are the third-culture children – those born in one country and brought up within another. Their cultural identity will not be with either of these cultures and so is perceived as a third culture. Often their cultural identity will be with other third-culture children, rather than with either their birth culture or their host culture. Many will have returned to the home country at some stage for education and, while appearing to be of this culture but having little understanding of it, will have found this to be a deeply alienating experience. For many it will feel natural to live in the culture of the country that they have grown up in, and they would need a really strong sense of vocation to be 'sent' to the culture that they were born into!

One week I interviewed two different single people, aged about 30, who came originally from other parts of the world, but who had spent the most recent half of their lives mainly in the UK. Both were open about influences shaping them both from UK culture and from their parents' culture. When asked about relationships with those of the opposite sex, one concluded that marriage could only be within his ethnic group whereas the other was open to marriage outside her ethnic group. I felt that this gave a useful pointer as to whether UK or parental cultural influences were stronger.

Cross-cultural understandings of vocation

An exciting theological insight for me, during my time in East Africa, was to find out from a Maasai farmer that only the shepherd could tell the difference between sheep and goats. It gave me a whole new understanding of the parable of the sheep and the goats and challenged my assumptions, based upon UK farms, that there are far more sheep than goats, that sheep and goats are kept separately and that any fool can tell them apart! Our cultural perspective will give us different gospel insights. Although this example is based upon a purely physical difference there can be many differences in Christian understanding due to culture.

I once had the experience of coming across theological comments, within an application form of an ethnically Indian Christian, that resonated with a Hindu understanding of karma or predestination.

In subsequent discussion with others involved in that selection process, we concluded that it is probably easier to recognize the way that culture shapes Christianity within other cultures than it is to see it within our own culture; to see the speck in the other's eye, rather than the beam in our own! This does not mean that it isn't there within our own culture.

I gather that it is fairly common in India to find that people are involved in Christian ministry because their parents dedicated them to God at an early age. Often the dedication to God was in response to God answering a childless couple's prayer for a baby. Personally I really struggle with such a commitment by the parents as being the basis for a person offering himself or herself to God's service later in life. I would have all sorts of questions about someone trying to live out someone else's aspirations and about an unhealthy control going on within the child's life. I would also want to explore issues to do with guilt. Yet despite all of my feelings I do need to concede that such a calling is grounded in a biblical model: the story of Samuel (1 Sam. 3). One only needs to read a Jane Austen novel to see that within certain UK families less than 200 years ago, the oldest son would expect to inherit all of the family property, the second oldest was expected to become a soldier and the next a clergyman. My hesitations probably come more from my Western sense of individualism than from a biblical perspective.

During a workshop I was running recently in Singapore, I was asked about people being called through dreams. In the world I inhabit, God does not 'do' dreams; having interviewed thousands of people, I have very rarely heard of a vocation being based upon a dream. Yet biblically dreams have much going for them as the basis of a calling. I am also aware that in some parts of the world many of those who convert from another faith to Christianity do so, in part, because of a dream. I think that if a dream has been part of the conversion experience then it would not be surprising if it also played a major part within the sense of calling.

In both of these cases it is important to have an understanding of the bigger picture and of how other Christians within that culture might express their sense of vocation. We need to accept that there is a tremendous breadth of biblical understanding and that different cultures will look more naturally to different parts of the Bible. Having said that, we should still ask the questions that come from our own (Western) perspective. It can be too easy, when encountering for the first time spiritual phenomena such as dreams or bargains with God, to back off and not to consider the other relevant factors.

> **Reflect . . .**
>
> Have any cross-cultural interviews challenged your theological assumptions? Have you been able to separate out which of your own assumptions are biblical, and which are cultural?

Cross-cultural within the UK

It is very easy for a UK organization to base its selection processes on the assumption that 'cross-cultural' is found in other countries and that the UK is a mono-culture. I only need to spell out the assumption for it to be recognized as false. Many UK-based agencies will have been shaped with the assumption that, if applicants have been born within the UK, they will be white, middle class and educated. However, if so, their processes will often struggle to appropriately test the vocation of those who are not these things.

Being part of a minority will, understandably, give one a different perspective on life to those of the majority community, as will the aspirations that are present within a middle-class educated family compared with a family in which there are no expectations of further education and in which a vocation would be considered a luxury for those who are in control enough of their lives to be able to make choices about what they do.

Practicalities

There are certain practicalities to consider when interviewing cross-culturally.

Paperwork

If the paperwork for a particular selection process has evolved as the best way to be able to assist the process for applicants from one particular culture, then it should not be surprising if it does not work so well for applicants from another culture. If your organization has used a particular application form for a number of years and found that most applicants responded to questions in a particular way and gave answers of a certain length and depth, it's easy to assume that there is something wrong with the applicant, rather than the paperwork, if the answers do not fit your expected pattern. Interestingly, it is often educational attainment, and whether the applicant studied within an educational system modelled upon the UK one, that determines how well an application form appears to work for a candidate.

Sometimes the questions used on forms might lose their clarity when read within a different culture and this can have an impact upon the answers. Some applicants may feel unable to share of themselves deeply to the anonymous reader of an application form, but may be perfectly happy to share deeply in person to an interviewer.

You should also be aware that some applicants may be completing the paperwork in their second or even third language, which could in itself put them at a disadvantage.

References

Often people from other cultures will depend upon references from people of their own culture. Such references may be written in a different style from that of references from within our own culture. If a reference is perceived to be either 'thin' or glowing, rather than balanced, then it is easy to blame this on the applicant, rather than on the reference writer. In truth, most references do tell you much more about the writer than the applicant.

Language barriers

My language ability is such that I would only ever use English as the medium for my questions and the anticipated answers. If you are interviewing someone for whom English is not the first language, it is helpful to identify where English fits within the person's language ability. To explore what language they think and process information in, and the differences they perceive that there are between thinking in that language and in English, can be a helpful step in our own understanding; it is also an acknowledgement that we recognize that there could be the possibility of both miscommunication and misunderstanding.

Same-sex interviews

Although it is not always possible it is far more appropriate for cross-cultural, one-to-one interviews to be conducted by someone of the same sex (for more on this see p. 100).

Confidentiality

I find that those I interview from my own culture rightly expect that information gathered about them will be treated as confidential and that sensitive information will be used only for the purpose for which it has been gathered. Apart from the fact that this is good practice, European Union legislation and the Data Protection Act makes the record-keeping aspect of this a legal requirement (for more on this see p. 76). Such an understanding of confidentiality will not always be found within other cultures. In part, this might be because the Christian community is quite small and everyone either knows everyone else or knows someone who knows the person, but it may also be because confidentiality is not understood or respected in the same way in different cultures.

I am sure that I hear far more sensitive information now than I did ten or 20 years ago. While this could possibly be because I am a more practised interviewer, it is probably because people, particularly younger people (as mentioned in Chapter 3), are prepared to be more open in sharing their vulnerabilities and weaknesses. Such openness can be infectious and has spread to some members of the older generations within the UK.

In a culture that does not have a real understanding of confidentiality people will be far more wary about what information they disclose and will not feel that it is appropriate to disclose confidential information about themselves. I have memories of one Asian family with whom it took several interviews before the more sensitive questions ceased to be avoided and were, in fact answered. I also have memories of another family that felt it was right to withdraw from selection processes rather than answer sensitive questions. At the time I assumed that there was some issue that they did not want us to explore; as my cross-cultural understanding has developed I have concluded that the problem was probably the depth of the interviewing process, rather than a specific issue.

Family dynamics

I remember rereading Genesis 12 and making the fascinating discovery that when Abram set off on his vocation into the great unknown he actually took all of his support systems with him; his whole extended family with the addition of servants, slaves and animals, accompanied him. From a western perspective it is easy to think primarily in terms of the nuclear family, with perhaps just a brief thought for non-dependent parents, siblings, nephews and nieces and so on. In other parts of the world, the pastoral and financial expectations that parents have of their children, in particular oldest sons, can be far greater. Some candidates may have gone to great lengths to escape from parental influences.

Loss of face

I can still remember much of the detail of several sermons I heard preached 20 years or so ago by the then Bishop of Woolwich, the Rt Revd Peter Hall. The secret to his preaching was to base it upon a story that was told against himself, and draw out some deep significant Christian conclusion. I remember most of the conclusions, and I still remember all of his stories; I find this a helpful communication tool. I was aware, while telling stories, at my own expense in Singapore, that what I was doing was countercultural – possibly this helps even more as a learning tool!

In some cultures it is not appropriate for someone to say or ask something that leads to loss of face. A similar idea is developed by Vincent Donovan in his discussion of what is meant by 'truth'.[21] In the West, we understand truth to be about facts; in other cultures truth will be about relationships. The worst thing to do is to damage the relationship. A simple example is given through the stranger, on foot, asking the local person whether it is far to a particular place. Obviously the stranger is hot and tired and does not want to hear the answer 'yes' – this could break the relationship – so the answer 'no' is given instead. Had the questioner asked the distance, rather than asking if it was far, the answer could have been both true to the fact and to the relationship.

So, for example, if you are interviewing and you want to explore experiences of failure, how these have been coped with and what has been learnt from them, but you think the candidate might not want to lose face, you should avoid the use of the word 'failure'.

Instead, your questions can focus upon the positive experience of learning from life's experiences. Although this will take longer, it should identify appropriate episodes for further exploration. After the candidate has spoken about his or her positive experience of learning, it will be easier to explore exactly how the episode was dealt with without the same risk of loss of face.

Different spiritual emphases

I believe that people from some cultures are more likely to give a spiritual answer to a question than those from my own culture are. Feeling comfortable with the balance between spiritual and rational understanding that is the norm within my own culture, I perceive them as over-spiritualizing issues. Of course, from their perspective, I must be under-spiritualizing!

In one particular case, I was concerned about what I saw as confusion between psychiatric health and spiritual warfare; I am not denying the existence of spiritual warfare, but my understanding is that if medication is being prescribed by a doctor, and taken by the patient, their condition should be understood as a medical, not a spiritual, issue. When I shared my concern with someone else from that culture about these boundaries being blurred, they asked why this was a problem. It made me realize that what I considered as over-spiritualizing was, in fact, a normal perspective within that culture and that I needed to make judgements from that perspective, rather than from mine.

Motivation

I sometimes received enquiries from those living in developing countries who told me that they felt that God was calling them to work in the UK, the USA or Japan. Being used to considering those who were prepared to make material sacrifices for their vocation, I felt that a sense of calling from a developing country to a developed country raised different questions that needed to be asked about motivation. However, articulating this conclusion also helped me to realize that there can be some very mixed motives for the person who is feeling called from the developed to the developing country; is there a need to be needed?

Christian diversity

When I interview those from the UK who are considering service overseas, I want to make sure that they realize that, in many countries, Christians do not drink alcohol and if they go to that country they would be expected not to do so either. Conversely, interviewing those from a culture where alcohol is taboo, there is a need to explore how candidates would be able to cope with working and worshipping with Christians who do drink alcohol. Once, when I had discussed this issue with candidates on a cerebral level, I found that during their visit to the project they were being considered for, they had been taken to a staff meeting in the local pub, and so the issue had been explored at a far more experiential level!

Many Christians living outside the West will be used to a more definite understanding of what is, and is not, acceptable Christian behaviour. They are less likely to have encountered the diversity of views that might be found within the West. Depending upon the context, issues of how they would cope with this might need exploration.

Institutionalized cultural prejudice

If a selection process has evolved as the best way to be able to assist the assessment of applicants from one particular culture, then it should not be surprising if it does not work so well for applicants from another culture. If there is such a mismatch, then intuitively we may feel that there is something wrong but not be able to articulate what it is and so project it on to the applicant. If the applicant feels that the process is not working well, his or her confidence can then easily become undermined. If you are processing people from other cultures, it is important to have people of other cultures involved in your selection processes, not only as interviewers, but also to engage critically with the processes.

Getting the balance right

Partly because there can be issues that begin to get us in touch with our own prejudices and partly because our inability to select those from other cultures can be a judgement upon our organization, there can sometimes be an attempt to over-compensate within our processes. Positive prejudice can be just as dangerous as negative prejudice (see Chapter 10).

The book *Too Valuable to Lose*[22] explores different causes of why people drop out of missionary work, and makes comparisons between the 'old sending countries' (e.g. the countries of Europe and North America, Australia and New Zealand) and the 'new sending countries' (e.g. Brazil, Korea and Singapore). Understandably the missionaries from old sending countries are from a far broader age range, and issues connected with parental care and children's education are a major cause of them leaving missionary work. Another major reason is lack of job satisfaction. From our generational understanding we can see that this is more of a concern for those born between 1945 and 1965, and again this issue would be expected to feature within the older age band of the older sending countries.

In comparison, the key issues leading to those from the new sending countries leaving missionary work are call, spiritual life, unresolved personal issues and relationships. These issues are all ones that can easily be spiritualized. If it is felt that God has strongly 'called', then there can be an assumption that any unresolved personal issues and relationships are no longer problems; an assumption that if God is calling, then he has already dealt with the issues, or healed the problem. Helping the candidate to identify the issue and to begin to deal with it might be the beginning of a healing process. The above analysis does, however, remind us of the importance of making sure that relationship and emotional problems are properly investigated and that real evidence is gained that issues have been resolved and that the sense of call is properly explored, and spiritual words are unpacked to find out what is really being expressed.

In summary, I would suggest the following ways of improving cross-cultural selection.

1 Use interviewers with cross-cultural experience and an understanding of cross-cultural communication.
2 Try to use interviewers from the culture or cultures involved; their understanding of the issues that shape life within that culture will give them insights into what questions to ask and how to ask the questions in an appropriate way. Don't be afraid to ask

these interviewers how you should explore particular issues sensitively within their culture.

3 Make sure that your interviewers include people from more than one culture. This will stop you falling into a 'them and us' mentality. Knowing that what they say will be heard by an interviewer of another culture should sharpen the mind of interviewers in making their report and help them to avoid simple cultural stereotypes.

4 Find ways to avoid miscommunication:

(a) If you are interviewing someone in a language that is not his or her first language, then check that you are speaking at a speed, and in a manner, that enables you to be clearly understood.

(b) Clearly indicate changes of topic and clarify the topic that you are focusing upon.

(c) Be aware that much communication is non-verbal and be aware of body language that might indicate that miscommunication is occurring (see Chapter 11).

(d) In the light of the above, allow longer for the interview.

Part 3
BEFORE INTERVIEWING

7

Tools of the trade 1: paperwork

Although most of the rest of this book concentrates upon interviewing, other resources also help with selection processes.

Providing information about your organization

None of us likes to apply for something and then be turned down or rejected; far better that we don't apply or that we decide at some point not to take our application further. This way we feel that we are in control of what is going on and are decision-takers and making the running. I always preferred it when a potential candidate made the decision not to go ahead and explained that decision to me, to when I made the decision and had to explain it to the person.

With this in mind, it is worth giving careful consideration to what initial information is sent out when someone makes an enquiry, and the impression that this gives. This initial information should resonate with those who you wish to apply, but make those who might not be appropriate begin to reflect upon whether they really have a calling to your agency. If your organization has a particular theological position then it is important to state it and so have potential applicants conclude that you don't fit them, rather than you concluding that they don't fit you. If you have a particular position on issues related to sexuality, it is worth stating this so that those who might be excluded can make that decision themselves. However, you may also wish to consider what it says about your church or organization if the only issue you have a position on is sexuality!

You can also include information about what would happen at each stage of the process and how long it will take. Those seeking a faster process, or a process that does not include such a thorough exploration of a particular issue, such as child protection checks, would be able to decide not to take their enquiry further.

Reflect . . .

Look through your literature. Does it give you a clear idea of:

- what your ministry is?
- your selection criteria?
- the ethos of your organization?
- the timescale for selection?
- training requirements?
- any financial requirements or implications?

Try looking at material from other organizations and see what they include in their literature that you omit. Would it be helpful to include such information?

First interviews

It's helpful to let candidates know what to expect when they attend a first interview. You could produce a leaflet headed 'The Initial Interview' giving answers to potential questions that candidates may have before coming to meet you for the first time. This document could explain what issues might be explored, and why, and give an indication of the depth of exploration that might be expected.

Reflect . . .

What would candidates need to know to prepare themselves for a first interview with your organization?

You should consider including the following information:

- Is your organization looking for a particular type of person?
- How will the candidate's 'call' or motivation be understood?
- What else is explored at interviews?
- Does your organization have a particular theological perspective?
- Does your organization have a particular stand on issues related to lifestyle?
- What happens after the interview?

This information can be sent out with initial forms (see below) so that those who feel uncomfortable with what would be covered within an interview, or with the depth of the interviews, can make their own decision not to proceed with their enquiry.

Types of forms

Most organizations use two distinct forms that the candidate will complete at different stages within the process. The first form might be known as an enquiry form, an initial form or a registration form. Usually the second form is the official application form and this is only completed after initial interviews.

Reflect . . .

Look at the forms that you use. What are you trying to achieve with each form? Do they achieve these purposes?

Initial forms

One purpose of the initial form is to help the agency make a decision as to whether or not they are going to meet the applicant. One of the most confusing things that can happen to candidates is to be invited for an interview and then to be told that they cannot move forward because of something that was obvious from the initial form. They won't believe you! They will be sure that the real reason is because of some other conclusions that you have come to, as a result of meeting them, that you are not prepared to share with them. This will be confusing and painful for them, and embarrassing for you.

If there are criteria such as age, educational attainments, marriage status, baptism or confirmation or church membership, or length of time within their current church, that will make a difference as to whether you begin the process, then make sure that such questions are on the form. It is to be hoped that, if you have explained the criteria in literature that you have previously sent out, you will not have many people completing forms who are not appropriate for a first interview.

You may wish to ask questions to find out about candidates' spiritual journey. Some organizations will ask for a brief description of this with the accompanying paperwork. There are obvious advantages in doing this but generally the answer will sound more real when narrated naturally, rather than written down.

This initial form will also help you to structure your initial interview. You will want to think what will be helpful in doing this. I found it helpful to be able to build up a chronological picture of what candidates had done during their life. Information about education and career, which encourages a chronological response, together with dates, is helpful. Sometimes there will be gaps and it can be helpful to be aware of these, so that they can be explored.

People's vocation can and should be built upon far more than just their educational attainments and profession; it is important to get a picture of hobbies, other interests, church and mission involvement, voluntary work, and community and political involvement so that you can explore what energizes and inspires the candidate. At an obvious level, you will want to contact the applicant and therefore need to have information about address, phone numbers and email. You will also want to know how readily you can contact someone, whether he or she would be compromised by being rung at work and whether a mobile phone or landline is the best means of contact.

For people applying to agencies in the UK, the information that is held about them is governed by the Data Protection Act 1998. It is helpful to put a statement on your forms explaining why you are holding information, assuring them that it will not lead to mailing for other purposes and informing them how long you will hold their information for. (For more on the Data Protection Act see p. 162.)

The application form

During the selection process, you will be making conclusions about candidates in your own words and getting the opinions of referees, which will be in the words of that referee; the application form is an opportunity to get information about candidates in their own words, rather than in the words of the interviewer or reference writer. It can be an opportunity to encourage them to reflect upon some of their experiences and aspirations and how these relate to their faith. If the application form is completed after preliminary interviews, it is unlikely that you will use the application form to make conclusions about the candidate; rather it will give you information in order to help you formulate further questions at the final interview stage. The form should be designed with this in mind. It can be helpful to look at the questions that other agencies use and to try to work out which ones could be useful within your own processes. The danger of this approach is that you could end up with an application form that is too long. You could ask other organizations which of their questions they find most helpful.

Real life . . .

An Anglican mission agency asked whether the candidate has any problems with any aspect of Anglicanism. They found that the non-Anglicans always answered 'no' and the Anglicans, without fail, answered 'yes'!

Of course, on reflection, this makes sense. If your church membership shows that you are committed to a denomination then, in saying that you have some problems, you are also saying that you can stick with it and be committed to it despite its failings. If you do not belong to that denomination and indicate that you have problems with that denomination then it begs the question as to why you are making such an application in the first place.

The deeper point is that particular questions can have different implications depending on where people are coming from, and it is worth bearing this in mind.

What to ask and what not to ask

There are some issues, such as criminal records and history of abuse, that it is inappropriate to record on forms. While I feel it is appropriate to ask about marital status on an initial form I would not ask questions about sexuality. As far as I know I have only had one enquirer lie about her marital status. It was when I sensitively asked how long ago she was widowed, so that I could explore the grieving process, that her blank look gave way to comprehension and she explained that she had said she was widowed (rather than divorced) on the form to make sure that she got interviewed. The woman was Scandinavian and it wasn't the done thing to ask such questions on initial forms there!

Doctrinal statements and doctrinal questions

Personally, I don't find asking doctrinal questions on forms to be very helpful because it tends to encourage model answers that will not always reflect reality. For example, a question about the Trinity is likely to encourage an answer that mentions and affirms the role of each person within the Trinity. Asking questions that relate faith to life might show that the faith is, in reality, focused upon only one person within the Trinity.

Doctrinal statements give an organization an opportunity to state what it believes and for those who wish to join that organization to decide if they can affirm the statement and join it. Obviously, candidates who wish to join the organization will wish to affirm the statement of faith even if it is not quite what they would want to say themselves. Be aware that some statements of faith were written to denounce a heresy of a particular age, and they can give the impression that it is the denouncement of that heresy, rather than belief in the living Christ, that is at the centre of their belief.

References and referees

References can be notoriously unhelpful. Despite this, there are ways of improving the quality of information that comes from them.

When to call for references

Increasingly, in the secular world, references appear to be called for after the job has been offered. Such references can offer very little to the selection process, and even though the job has been offered subject to references, it is very difficult to change the selection decision at that stage. It is inappropriate for a candidate to ask people to be referees until their enquiry becomes a definite application, so a good time to ask for references is before the final interview stage. This allows their use in helping to decide which areas and issues need further exploration at final selection and how to explore such issues. As I argue in Chapter 5, references are assumptions, and further exploration is needed to get the information into the open domain, so that both we and the candidate are aware of the facts.

Who to ask for references

It's a good idea to try to keep some control over who provides references by talking this through with the candidate at the initial interview, before the formal application form is submitted. Try finding referees who can tell you more about the candidate's work, faith and personality, including any general issues. Although there are three main areas to cover, it's worth asking for more than three referees to make sure that all the areas are fully covered. You can explain to candidates that references are not a hurdle to be cleared, but additional pieces of information to help guide the decision.

Some people are, naturally, very hesitant about asking for a reference from their current employer; the employer could easily assume that the employee is not committed to the current role. Usually there will be previous employers who can be approached and also current colleagues who can comment, even if not from the position of line manager. When testing Christian vocation, we are often interviewing people who are coming from areas of work where we do not have the professional expertise to assess their working ability accurately, and so references can often be crucial in finding out whether they are good at their job or not.

Sometimes we are interviewing people who have come recently from a course of study, either a professional course or a Bible college course, so we can also call for a tutor's reference to supplement the professional reference, or to replace it if there is no working experience.

You may be involving the candidate's church more deeply in the process (which is covered in the next chapter), but the minimum must be to ask them for a reference. It is important to ask the person who is responsible for the congregation for the reference. Sometimes that person will not know the candidate well and will therefore delegate this task to a colleague, an elder or a house group leader. Fair enough; but it is their decision to delegate this task. You will know that the reference is coming with the authority of the church leader, even if written by someone else; you will also know that the church leader and not the candidate has chosen who should write the reference. Even a church leader who has not been with a congregation for long should be able to delegate this task to an appropriate person if necessary.

Clergy move on from time to time and sometimes it will be appropriate to call for a reference from the previous church leader. If so, then this can be supplemented by someone else with some authority who is still part of the candidate's current church.

People can frequently change jobs and churches, and work and church references may well be written by people who have not known the candidate for long. It is therefore worth asking for a reference from someone who has known the candidate in a personal capacity for a while. Rather than specify a particular number of years – which, according to age, could represent very different stages in the person's life, you could ask for someone who has known the candidate for a certain length of time – perhaps for a quarter of his or her life. This should mean that the referee has witnessed change and growth in the candidate's life.

Sometimes a referee will not be able to answer certain sections of the reference form. Rather than take a candidate to final selection without this information, which could easily prejudice the interviewers, you can try to get the candidate to identify an additional referee who can provide this information.

Style of reference

If you write a letter to referees and outline the particular issues that you wish them to comment on, you might find some referees just go through and write yes or no on your letter and return it to you! It's more helpful to provide a form for referees to complete. Apart from clearly seeing the information that is given, it is also easy to spot the information that is not given. As well as questions covering the relevant issues, you can also ask if there was any reason why it would not be wise to accept the person and whether there is any other relevant information that they wish to give.

It is helpful to stress to the referee that you are not selecting competitively, but that you have the candidate's best interest at heart. This can then be followed by a reminder of the stresses of the work and an encouragement that honest answers are in the best interests of the applicant.

Phone calls to referees

Sometimes there will be comments or gaps on the reference form that will be worth following up with a phone call. To enable this, it is worth asking at the end of the form if it is possible to ring and if so when and on what number. Some companies will have policies forbidding referees to provide any additional information in this way, so as to make sure that any information or opinion expressed about an employee is on file in case of litigation.

Occasionally different referees will give very different perspectives on the same areas of the candidate's life, and you may seriously wonder if they are writing about the same person. In such cases a phone call to one, or both, of the referees can help to clarify the reasons for their different perspectives. If there are comments coming from a phone call that cast light upon particular issues, then it will be important to make a clear note in the file of such issues to supplement the reference.

Some references, sadly, will tell you far more about the reference writer than the candidate!

Legalities

Increasingly, employers are becoming concerned about the legal implications of writing references and the possibilities of being sued, either by employees who have not been offered a job, or by employers who blame the reference writer for their decision to offer employment to someone who does not meet their standards. As a result of this, some employers have introduced policies that restrict the information provided within references to a bare minimum of factual information that can be proved in court by reference to the employee's file.

Although the employer is not obliged to show a person the reference that they have written, a candidate can ask to see the file that you hold, which includes references. Although I have never had a candidate ask to see his or her file or read the references, there is a strong possibility that the whole culture of reference writing will change so that references will come to have limited value.

Confidentiality

Even without the legal issues, references can provide you with certain dilemmas. I was asked once by a vicar whether the candidate might ever see what he had written in his reference. He said that this would not change what he wanted to say, but he felt the need to be prepared to handle this if this was the case. If you are asked a similar question you need to explain that yes, a candidate could ask to see the file, including the references.

If candidates tell you something within an interview or on an application form, they know that you know it, and you can easily raise the issue at further interviews. If the issue has only been brought to light from a reference, then you will have a dilemma about how to indicate that you know about the issue without breaking the confidence of the referee. In the case that I referred to above, of the vicar asking whether the candidate might ever see the reference, the reference confirmed impressions that had been gained in earlier interviews and so those interviews could be used as the basis for exploring the issue further. In other cases there may be a need for a conversation with the referee so that you can discuss together how such confidentialities are handled. Possibly the referee will need to be open with the candidate about what he or she have shared, and why. This whole issue is explored further in Chapter 13.

8

Tools of the trade 2: other resources

Reflect . . .

Apart from forms, references and interviews, how else might you find out about candidates? What type of information will you want to find out? How will you use that information?

The role of the home church

Mention is made in the previous chapter about references, and how they are used. As well as seeking written information from a church in the form of a reference, some organizations will want to engage more deeply with the home church and meet the church leadership as part of the selection process. Doing this affirms that vocation should be encouraged and nurtured by the local church. It not only provides an opportunity to discuss openly what is being said, and perhaps discover what is not being said, but also to explore how the church can support and affirm the candidate as he or she progresses through the process and engage with questions that the church might have about the whole process. In engaging with the local church, there are some factors worth bearing in mind.

The home church's own understanding of its role

Although God may call more people from some churches than from other churches, he is not restricted by the type of church that he calls people from. Some churches will provide many role models of those who have grown their vocation within that church and will have a strong emphasis upon encouraging and nurturing vocation; as a result they may have set up well-tried processes for this purpose and be very wary of people who don't fit into these processes. Other churches may be so excited if someone feels they may have a vocation that they will just shout 'Alleluia!' and pass them on to regional or national selection processes.

Depending upon the church's ecclesiology there will be different understandings of how much of the nurturing and testing of vocation should be the responsibility of the local church and how much should be the responsibility of regional or national structures. Churches with a more congregational ecclesiology will expect to take on a greater role than those that have a more episcopal ecclesiology. Some churches will see the local church as being the primary focus for all aspects of vocation whereas other churches will have an understanding that appreciates the regional and national focus and the emphasis on nationally recognized criteria and standards of selection.

The relationship between the home church and the selection organization

There might be a well-established relationship between the local church and the area or national selection processes, with a deep level of trust between the two. But occasionally previous events may have led to a lack of trust. If a candidate who has been strongly recommended by a church has not been accepted, then a church can sometimes wonder whether its candidates are viewed less favourably than other candidates.

The consideration of different generations in Chapter 3 helps us to understand that in years gone by there was a sense of loyalty to agencies, which meant that a candidate from a particular church was likely to approach one of just a few well-known agencies to explore his or her vocation. If the vocation is within the ministry of a particular denomination, then there is probably only the one agency to explore the vocation with. If the vocation is to cross-cultural mission, there might be many possibilities. People today are far more likely to approach the agency that best matches the specific skills that they are offering than one that has traditionally been linked to their church, so often there will be a new relationship for the local church, rather than the church and agency being familiar with each other.

How well is the candidate known?

The level of knowledge of candidates can vary hugely within different churches. Often the knowledge of the candidate is at a social level rather than being pastoral or spiritual, unless there has been a specific episode that has required a pastoral or spiritual engagement. I have regularly asked candidates about their patterns of Bible study and prayer and how they sustain and grow their spiritual lives; you can probably assume that not many clergy will have such detailed information about their members.

The size of a church can be a factor that limits the leadership's knowledge of a candidate, but a house group or cell group system would mean that someone within the structures of the church will have a deeper understanding that can be fed into the church's understanding of the candidate.

Candidates who are exploring a Christian ministry should have taken on responsibilities within their home church, and their church leadership should have an understanding of how they relate their pastoral and spiritual gifts to such tasks. Their sense of vocation should also have been explored with their church leadership at a preliminary stage, before the approach to a regional or national selection process.

Knowledge of behaviour and background

The home church will have a knowledge of how the candidate functions, and will have seen him or her function in various different situations and circumstances. The church won't necessarily have the more detailed knowledge of the candidate's life story or know of the ups and downs of life that have resulted in these different patterns of behaviour, but they will know the reality of the candidate's contribution to the church and the quality of his or her relationships and ability to sustain relationships. They might also have observed how the candidate has coped with grief, stress, success and failure.

Nurture or testing

As mentioned in Chapter 2, it is helpful if there is a different person, and emphasis, when the focus changes from nurturing to testing vocation. Some churches will be able to handle this change of role, but most appreciate the more objective role of regional or national selection processes at this stage.

Objectivity or affirmation

Sometimes it is not easy for a local church to be objective; perhaps they do not have the skills to switch from being pastorally affirming to objectivity, or perhaps they are afraid of the consequences of being honest. It is not impossible for someone totally inappropriate to feel encouraged by their church when, in fact, many of the congregation have doubts and concerns, each finding it difficult to be the lone voice that raises those concerns. Some churches will develop structures to begin to test vocation and such structures should provide a more objective scrutiny of the sense of vocation.

What is 'church' for Generation X and beyond?

Few Christians would argue with the fact that to be a Christian you need to be part of, and committed to, the Body of Christ – the Church. Traditionally, that has meant belonging to a local congregation; occasionally it has meant belonging to a congregation near the work place – after all much of life is lived out in the work place. 'Home church' used to mean a local church, but the combination of people becoming more mobile and churches increasingly focusing the emphasis of their ministry is that, more and more, people will travel greater distances to belong to a church that meets their needs or the needs of their family. For some Christians, commitment might result in being involved, in different ways, in two churches. Generation X are a highly mobile generation who can move job and home frequently and who may not fit the criteria to belong fully to their home church.

I can think of a few good long-term candidates who had moved away from their family's church, aged 18, to go to a big student church at university and then spent a year or two overseas on a short-term programme before returning to study for an appropriate Masters degree that better qualified them to work overseas than in the UK. Having completed this degree, they then sought a temporary job, unrelated to their qualifications, and applied to return overseas for long-term service. Having seen them through a short-term programme, I was aware of their suitability, but which is their home church? Their parents' church, where they are still known although they haven't attended it regularly since they were 18? The big university church, where they spent three years, but which has seen hundreds more students pass through in the subsequent three years? The overseas church, where they spent two years? Or is it the university church that they went to occasionally, amid the pressures of study and catching up with family and friends again, during the year of studying for their Master's? Or the church they go to for a few months after completing their course, and while making their application?

There might be times when a good candidate cannot easily identify a church that would want to be able to affirm him or her as belonging to them and the support of which they would have while going through selection processes. In cases like the one given above, it can be worth making exceptions, but candidates do still need to be able to identify where, within the wider Body of Christ, they are getting the necessary pastoral and prayer support from.

'Ice-breakers' and team exercises

I think that the appropriateness of using either 'ice-breakers' or team exercises needs serious consideration. When I first joined CMS there used to be 'ice-breaking' exercises at residential selection conferences; it was believed that they would help candidates to relax and get to know each other and the interviewers within an informal activity. The first that I remember was when we provided Christian posters; candidates needed to choose one and say something about why they had chosen it. Apart from issues about whether you rushed to get a good poster, or behaved like a 'good Christian' and ended up with the one that no one else wanted, it is one of those exercises that, far from breaking the ice, can really 'freeze' people up at the beginning of a conference.

Later, we used simulation games instead. I can still remember the 45-minute discussion that selectors once had focusing upon whether a candidate had cheated or not and, if he had, what conclusions should be drawn? Did cheating indicate initiative or moral weakness? Either way, he turned out to be a good candidate.

The subsequent discussion about whether we should continue with ice-breaking exercises was far shorter! We concluded that if we didn't know what we were looking for with such exercises then the candidates would also be confused. We also concluded that an exercise is valid only if it has specific purposes and there are observers who are skilled in observing and analysing the exercise.

Real life . . .

A group of candidates was taken on a brief visit to a community project that they had applied to manage. They were each asked in turn to list the changes and improvements that they would make should they be appointed.

The sixth candidate, in a group of 12, perhaps feeling that all of the good ideas had been used up anyway, said he felt that the question was inappropriate: it wasn't the way he worked and he'd want to go into the project and take time to find out what had been tried in the past, what had worked and why, and then work with others on what the goals should be and how they might be achieved.

His response not only blew his chances of moving to the next stage of the selection process, but it rather spoilt the whole exercise! The six people who followed all needed to make a decision as to which way to jump, with some repeating the best of the initiatives that had already been mentioned and others indicating that they too would wish to consult before making suggestions.

An awkward candidate, even one with a very good point, can totally mess up an exercise and damage its validity.

If the selection process is competitive, then the purpose of the exercise is for candidates to show that they are the best, and it can be very difficult to draw valid conclusions. How do you judge if someone is good at enabling and affirming others? How do you distinguish between what the candidate has done, and what the people being 'enabled' did for themselves? I hope that you are not considering competitive processes in the testing of vocation, but the lessons drawn here may still be helpful.

The Ministry Division of the Church of England used an exercise in which each candidate was given a topic that he or she briefly introduced to the other candidates before chairing a discussion for a specified time and then summing up. Such an exercise gives an indication of how well a candidate can perform skills that are likely to be needed in ministry: chairing a meeting and summing up, as well as an ability to discuss a variety of relevant topics, are all relevant skills for clergy.

In an exercise like this it should be relatively easy for the selectors to agree on how well a candidate managed. But even here there are dangers: for example, if someone says something that borders on racism you may end up witnessing how everyone else copes with this comment and the remaining discussion may well be skewed. You also need to make sure that the skills you are assessing are relevant to the vocation: for example, this exercise probably wouldn't be the best one to use when assessing people who are considering overseas mission.

If exercises are used then the following needs to be borne in mind:

- exercises need to be designed to measure relevant skills, and this means that they are more likely to be relevant within a process that is selecting for a specific role, rather than for the breadth of roles that could be covered by mission partner selection;
- if exercises are used within a competitive setting then their purpose and validity need particular consideration;
- observers need to be clear about what they are trying to observe and measure and, if need be, trained in such observation; and
- an individual can thwart the exercise and damage the validity of it; if this happens, observers will then need to consider carefully whether any conclusions can be drawn in that particular instance.

Testing

Testing is very different from the use of exercises: it is an objective way of using well-researched tests for measurable attributes. The tester is not making subjective judgements, as can easily happen with an exercise, but is objectively comparing the candidate with other people who have completed the test in the past. Some tests can be bought 'over the counter', but testers do need to be trained to carry them out so that they are aware of how they can and can't fit into a process and of their validity. The tester will be able to calculate a raw score but, in order to make sense of this, they will need to compare the candidate with a wider 'population' and draw conclusions as to how the candidate compares with that wider population. For comments to be relevant, it will be important to draw comparisons with an appropriate grouping.

If you use the same tests for several years you will be able to draw up your own figures for your own population and compare a candidate with previous candidates. Usually this will be done by using percentiles; that is, looking at hundredths of the population. You are then able to comment that someone fits into, say, the top 10 per cent or the middle 40 per cent. It is also helpful to compare your results with the wider population as well; a score that is in the bottom 10 per cent for your own population might still be considered average for the larger population.

Tests may not always be a good indicator of someone's capability in a vocation. For example, a person who has not worked professionally for many years because of caring for children or other dependants may not do well on some tests but might be perfectly suitable for the post being applied for. You would need to try and compare such a person's score with the results of similar people, which may not always be practical or possible.

Tests fall into two different types of categories: ability tests and psychometric tests.

Ability tests

There are some tests that look at reasoning ability, which can be considered to have four elements: general, mathematical, abstract and spatial. We might expect that academic results will give an indicator as to reasoning ability. There are various reasons why this is not always the case.

- Most school subjects focus upon general or mathematical reasoning, with abstract reasoning playing a minor role and spatial reasoning only being found within a small minority of subjects.
- Increasingly, dyslexia is being recognized at an early age but there are still plenty of people whose academic results were blighted by dyslexia.
- Academic results might depend more upon either hard work or a desire to learn, rather than on reasoning ability.
- Some people have done badly at exams because of major events such as bereavement or family splits that were going on in their lives at the time.

- Some exam systems might favour a particular culture or academic style so that those who are different score badly. The same might also be true of some reasoning tests.

If your ministry, or the training for your ministry, demands a particular level of reasoning ability then, bearing in mind the above comments, ability tests can be a useful tool so that you are not just dependent upon how candidates previously performed at school and college.

Psychometric tests

Psychometric tests measure psychological factors. They can be useful tools but can also very dangerous in the wrong hands, and training should be rigorous. Certain tools are not valid ones for selection.

As mentioned earlier, because it is based upon Jungian rather than Freudian psychological understandings, Myers-Briggs assessment has become very popular in Christian circles. Myers-Briggs is a very helpful tool, but it is not a selection tool and must never be used in this way. With Myers-Briggs, many people will function better on their 'shadow' side (i.e. the indicator that is not their preferred way of functioning) than another person might function within one of their preferences.

Certain psychometric tests will work with certain cultures but may not be valid within another culture. The manual that comes with the test should give an idea of the different groupings and populations that have been considered in validating scores and show whether it is a tool that will work outside the culture where it was developed.

I am aware of three agencies that use or have used psychometric tests as part of their selection processes. Two of these agencies pragmatically chose a test because they had someone who was already trained to administer the particular test. There doesn't appear to be any one test that has been recognized as being particularly helpful in the testing of Christian vocation. If you do choose to use a psychometric test, it is essential that it is one that is designed for selection purposes, rather than one that is designed purely for counselling or to enable better understanding of roles within a team.

Although ability tests and psychometric tests can give helpful information it is unwise to let them have the final say upon a subject. They should be used as an objective way of helping to identify issues that can be explored further through interviews.

Psychiatric or psychological screening

In my years of interviewing, I have noticed a significant change in the backgrounds of those that I interviewed. No longer do all of the candidates come from stable secure family backgrounds. Often there was trauma in the family background or in the life of the candidates themselves. Often it was because of God's grace breaking into their life through the trauma that they were exploring their vocation.

Such events might make a candidate particularly vulnerable when faced with the stresses of ministry or of another culture. Alternatively, working through these events might have helped him or her to have grown and matured beyond his or her years. Although you could hazard a guess as to which was true, it does need a professional really to answer such questions. You might find it helpful, with the candidate's permission, to provide the earlier interview reports to the professional conducting such screening; this provides some information and will allow some deeper digging within the time available.

It can be helpful to have such professional screening before the final selection stage; this means that the particular areas of vulnerability have already been covered and do not need to be explored by your interviewers. It will still be valid for an interviewer to explore, for example, the impact that the episode made upon faith or the ability to form relationships, but not to pass judgement upon those areas that require the input from the professional.

Professional screening is not cheap, but it is far cheaper than the financial costs of training someone for a vocation that he or she is not able to fulfil, let alone the spiritual and emotional costs of someone needing to drop out of a vocation because complex issues were not explored adequately.

Medical screening

I have come across examples of physical healing that I can only understand as being caused by God's healing touch. I have also come across people who feel that there has been healing when, in fact there has not been. Sadly, I have come across those whose sense of vocation has been part of an attempt to bargain with God: 'God, if you heal me then I will give my life to you through this particular ministry.'

It is important that with any testing of vocation medical checks are made to see whether the person is fit enough for the ministry and so that any necessary recommendations can be made about how and where that ministry is carried out. With short-term cross-cultural service, a knowledgeable medical agency can use medical forms, completed by the candidate's GP or the candidate, to screen candidates and then meet only those candidates for whom they need to follow up specific issues. With long-term cross-cultural service, it can be very helpful to arrange for the candidates to have a medical assessment with the medical agency; as well as providing a more rigorous medical screening, this also allows candidates to follow up any medical questions or concerns that they might have with someone qualified to answer such questions.

Financially, you will not want to have the costs, for you or the candidate, of medical screening at too early a stage within the process, before you know whether the candidate is really likely to go ahead. You will, however, want to ask about health at an early stage and, if any obvious health issues that could be contra-indicators – physical or psychiatric – come up at this early stage, it will be worth exploring them early within the process.

Protection policies for children and vulnerable adults

Sadly, some parts of the Church have a very bad reputation on the whole issue of the protection of children and vulnerable adults. It is essential that every organization develops its own policy if it is taking on those who might work either with children or with vulnerable adults. Within many ministries this could be true of all those involved, so you may want a policy that applies to all candidates. Many procedures are just a police search conducted by the Criminal Records Bureau, but it is also a good idea to include separate questions to referees and a self-declaration form.

High-profile, national cases have shown that police checks will only work if allegations are recorded, candidates are unlikely to recommend as a referee someone who might know something that they are trying to keep from you, and people do not necessarily tell the truth on self-declaration forms. The fact that you have a policy, and that applicants know that you have a policy, should reduce the number of inappropriate people applying, but such processes are not foolproof. In-depth interviews are not likely to produce hard evidence but might well, for various reasons, make you wary. If someone has moved very frequently and not kept contact with those that he or she knew at these different times, even if each move has apparently been for a valid reason, it will be important to try to identify people who knew the person well at these different stages of life and to call for references from them, as well as for current references.

What do your processes say to the applicant?

A final consideration is the matter of what your processes say to your candidates. Admittedly, I didn't get very much feedback from those who started to explore their vocation with CMS and then chose to go with another agency, but the feedback that I did get from those who had come part way, or all the way, through these processes was that they appreciated an organization that really wanted to know who they were. They appreciated the thoroughness of the selection process and, if they were told what would happen and why and believed that we were on their side and trying to help them determine what God wants of them, they were very positive about the selection processes.

9

An interviewing strategy

Confidentiality

I know a lot of very exciting and encouraging facts about what has happened in many people's lives; I also know a lot of information that I wish I didn't. All the information that I have been given has been for a purpose and I have been given it on the basis that I respect the confidential nature of the information and treat it with the respect and confidence that it demands.

The success of any selection process depends upon the respect that those who go through it have for the process. Much of this respect will depend upon the ability of the selection process to deal with confidentialities. If people believe that confidences will be respected they are likely to share sensitive information; if they have heard stories of confidences being passed on they will be very wary of sharing deeply of themselves. If people do not share willingly and fully about themselves, you will not be gaining the evidence that you need to make good selection decisions, and your selection process will become compromised.

> **Reflect . . .**
>
> What do you do if you find that someone has been sexually abused by someone who was, and still is, in a position of trust?
>
> What do you do if you find out that the candidate has sexually abused someone in the past?

It is far better to develop policies on issues of sexual abuse before you come across the situation, rather than in response to a specific case. It can be helpful to consult with other organizations when developing policies. Space does not allow me to address all of the issues here, but it is important that victims of sexual abuse are not made to feel guilty or that they are to blame. It is also important that if there is a risk of the abuser still abusing others then he or she is helped to bring this out into the open.

Generally, if a candidate is admitting pre-conversion illegal activities to you then, apart from any selection issues, you will want to consider your responsibilities as to whether the issue has been dealt with and whether the public is still at risk. If the issue is sexual abuse, I would not feel confident to make this judgement and would feel the need to address the issue. Having a child protection policy in place, and making candidates aware of the policy, makes it less likely that you will need to deal with such an issue, but it also gives you a greater mandate to get the issue out in the open if the need ever does arise.

If you interview for a small agency that is only recruiting personnel from a limited pool of applicants you will need to be more wary about who knows whom than you will if you work with a bigger agency. I have worked with some agencies in which at least one of the interviewers knew the candidate, the candidate's family or someone from the candidate's church. Occasionally, interviewers even find themselves interviewing those whom they had worked with as fellow interviewers! Generally, you should always try to set up interviews where the interviewers do not know the candidates, their families or members of their churches.

How many interviews?

Reflect . . .

How many interviews do you currently have within your processes? Does each have a specific purpose? What is each trying to achieve?

In Chapter 2 I stressed the importance of differentiating between encouraging, nurturing and testing vocation; each will need its own process with appropriate interviews. Interviews begin at the nurturing stage.

Nurturing vocation

If you are nurturing vocation then you will want to be reasonably assured that candidates are ready to have their vocation tested before allowing them to move on to that stage. This might mean there will be a minimum number of interviews, but the maximum number will be discretionary depending upon when the time is considered right to move to the final stage. Sometimes nurturing will involve setting up a number of interviews over quite a long period so that different aspects of vocation can be explored at each stage, and it might mean that candidates needs to work at their understanding of particular issues, through reading, and possibly through completing written assignments, or through gaining experiences, and not move on to the next stage until the previous stage has been completed.

Generally there will be a need for at least two interviews during this stage of the process, not only so that issues can be reflected upon further by the candidate, but also so that issues that arise from the first interview can be reflected upon by the interviewer and explored more fully at subsequent interviews. It is also helpful at this stage for more than one interviewer to engage with the candidate so that the decision to proceed to the next stage is based upon more than one person's assessment, and decisions are not confused by how well two personalities do, or do not, relate to each other.

Testing vocation

If the testing of vocation is to be seen as a decision that is made by the representatives of the Body of Christ then, for this to feel authentic, there will need to be more than one person involved within the process. There is also likely to be a lot of material to cover and one interview is unlikely to be able to do justice to this. It doesn't mean, however, that all of the representatives of the Body of Christ need to be involved in each stage of the process for each candidate.

It is also unlikely that only two interviewers will be adequate. If there are only two interviewers the main emphasis of the selection process will focus upon their comments and, if their views are different, selection decision can be distorted by the dynamics between the two interviewers concerned. Having three or more interviewers involved in the whole decision-making process gives scope for a healthy interplay within the selection dynamics and also allows each interview to focus upon different issues.

If you are testing the vocation of married couples you may also want to include a joint interview on issues that face them as a couple, as well as individual interviews.

How many interviewers in each interview?

Although you may still hear stories of organizations that have a dozen or so interviewers sitting around a table interviewing a candidate, fortunately this is now rare. Although some agencies have a preference for two interviewers, my own preference is for one-to-one interviews. One-to-one interviewing creates a deeper relationship between the candidate and leads to greater openness and real depth in what is shared. It is much more difficult for this relationship to develop if another interviewer is present.

If you are using two interviewers then it is important to clearly work out the role of each and how the dynamics will work. I remember an occasion when I was interviewing and whenever I left a pregnant pause before asking a really penetrating question my fellow interviewer, assuming I had finished, jumped in with his own question, and my moment was lost for ever. If you are going to interview as a pair, work out the ground rules: for example, one of you may explore an issue fully and then hand over the questioning on another issue to the other interviewer.

Alternating questioning can give the interviewers some space to reflect upon what they are doing and formulate future questions, but there is still a need to listen carefully to all that is being said in response to the other interviewer's questioning, and it can be even more difficult to make sense of the answer when it wasn't a question that you asked.

Each interviewer must check that the other has finished before concluding the interview.

Some agencies will have two interviewers involved but with one in a minor role, perhaps taking notes and observing the dynamics between the other interviewer and the candidate. This sounds attractive at one level, but of course the observer will also have an impact upon the dynamics, and someone sitting on the edge of things, as an observer, may make for a strained atmosphere. As an interviewer I would want to choose my words more carefully, and I am sure that the interviewee will probably not be as relaxed and open.

It could be argued that it is no longer appropriate to have two people alone in a room together as either the interviewer might take advantage of the candidate or the candidate might claim that this has happened. Although some thought needs to be put into this issue when different-sex interviews take place, many buildings have glass panels within the doors that should be reassuring to interviewer and interviewee alike, and such doors also stop interviews being interrupted by people coming in to see if the room is free! It is to be hoped that political correctness has not yet reached a stage where each interview needs a chaperone.

What is each interview trying to achieve?

It is important to think carefully what each interview is trying to achieve and what falls within its brief. Some agencies that use three separate interviews will have one that focuses primarily on professional issues and issues relating to that specific vocation, another that focuses upon relationships or pastoral issues, and a third that focuses primarily on faith and vocation. Other agencies that have clarified their selection criteria under a variety of different headings will allocate different criteria to each interview. Some agencies will combine a couple of such criteria in each interview in a way that makes sure that each criterion is covered by two different interviewers.

Although no agency is likely to be seeking those who live out their lives in three separate compartments, divisions need to be drawn somewhere; the best way to do this is to draw up guidelines for each type of interview used. A danger of such guidelines is that interviewers can feel that they need to explore every item within the guidelines even though some of the information has already been gathered through earlier interviews. Such guidelines are best used as a way of deciding which of the issues that should be explored rightly belongs to which interview. Sometimes an issue may need to be explored from different perspectives; for example, a particular episode may have had an impact upon faith, relationships and self-esteem and need to be explored from at least two of these perspectives.

Also, unless there is a prior agreement about which interviewer is exploring which issue, there can be a tendency for all interviewers to want to explore the 'interesting' issues, perhaps at the expense of more 'important' issues.

Who does which interview?

Some organizations will use the same interviewer to conduct one type of interview for every candidate. This has the advantage of consistency, with the same criteria being applied to everyone. However, if the process is not a competitive one, consistency is not as important as it might otherwise be. Selection processes will be most effective and less threatening if prior thought goes into who does which interview.

- With an interview that explores professional issues, try – whenever possible – to use an interviewer who has an idea about some of the relevant issues involved within that particular profession. There can be sensitivities in this area, however; for example, a nurse once explained to me that while nurses can interview doctors, doctors should never interview nurses! During the early days of women's ordination, there were specific sensitivities about ordained men interviewing ordained women, although this is probably less of an issue now. Be aware of where there could be hierarchical issues that could complicate the interview rather than shed light.
- Make sure that relationship issues are explored within a same-sex interview. Often people, particularly younger people, will speak quite openly about sensitive issues within a different-sex interview, but a same-sex interview is more likely to encourage such openness.
- If you are selecting candidates only from a particular part of the Christian spectrum, Christian diversity is unlikely to be a major issue, but if your candidates and interviewers represent theological diversity, then it can be helpful to put some thought into deciding whether some interviewers might be less comfortable with certain interviews and if certain candidates might feel that they have not been fully understood by some interviewers.

- If you are arranging interviews for married couples, the interviewer should be someone who is married and who would make realistic assumptions about marriage.

Interview timetables

Before an interview itself, interviewers will need to do serious preparation and make their own notes to structure the interview (see p. 118). Before each interview there will need to be time for the interviewers to remind themselves about who the candidate is and what the candidate has said about himself or herself, and to look again at notes. After each interview time needs to be allocated for making some brief notes before moving on to the next candidate. If each interview is of the same type, and similar issues are being explored, it will be even more important to feel that there has been some sort of closure on the material of one candidate before moving on to the next; the same will be true if candidates are similar in age or life experience.

A process that does not allow interviewers to prepare adequately beforehand and to feel there has been completion after seeing each candidate will not allow the interviewers to do justice to each candidate.

Setting the scene

Reflect . . .

What are the potential barriers to getting an interview off to a good start?

Various factors can influence how the interviewee feels at the outset of the interview. Anticipating these factors and setting the scene as you wish can help to get the best out of the interview. Here are some of the potential barriers and how they can be overcome.

- Expecting the candidates to find you and knock on the door of the room in which you are interviewing can bring back all sorts of memories of head teachers' studies or visits to the doctor. This can lead to the interviewee getting back in touch with the feelings associated with head teachers and doctors, and this doesn't necessarily bode well for getting the interview off to a good start. Instead, greet candidates at reception (preferably yourself) and then show them to the interview room.

- Having chairs of different heights will lead to one person looking down on the other and can confuse the dynamics; try to ensure that all the chairs offer the same level of comfort and are of the same height.
- Having a desk or a table between you and the candidate can create a barrier and, again, make it feel like a visit to the head teacher or the doctor. Instead, have a table to the side, which gives you somewhere to put papers, a cup of coffee or glass of water.
- Sitting the interviewee directly opposite you, and so forcing eye contact, can feel quite threatening; equally a seating arrangement that could cause a cricked neck for any eye contact to be possible is not a good arrangement either. An angle of about 20–30° can allow good eye contact without forcing it.
- Making candidates sit in a position where they have bright lights, either natural or artificial, shining into their eyes might prove effective in films in which the interrogator is giving the 'third degree' but, unless you wish to appear menacing, this is best avoided.
- Often ideal seating arrangements are not possible; if this happens then the best thing is to acknowledge it and point out that you are aware that it is far from ideal. This will at least mean that the interviewee knows that you are aware of the situation, and have not created it deliberately, and this should overcome much of the potential damage to the dynamics.
- If you have paperwork on the interviewee, it is good to acknowledge this and explain what paperwork you have. If the candidate has put work into completing a lengthy form or a written assignment, do acknowledge this and thank him or her for the work.
- If you have confidential material, such as references, it is best not to place these where they can be seen, even if they would have to be read upside down.
- If you explain exactly what is going to happen, how long the interview is likely to last and when questions can be asked (if

this is encouraged) then candidates are more likely to feel relaxed and in a position to open up and share with you. If they don't know when they can ask their questions, they might interrupt the flow of your interview by trying to ask these at the wrong time.

- I have heard some interviewers indicate that the interview is the place to try to put candidates into a difficult situation to see how well they cope. But the interview is an artificial situation and it would be better to explore some real occasions of difficulty and find out how they coped with these in the past. If you do use the interview to try to 'stress out' candidates, to measure their ability to cope, then the rest of the interview will also be acted out with an expectation of possible sudden stress, and you will not get the best out of your candidates.

Beginnings, endings and prayer

It is helpful to encourage candidates to feel relaxed at the beginning of the interview; this will enable them to feel comfortable and confident and to open up as the interview develops. This is best achieved by encouraging them to speak about something that is not threatening to them; so avoid trying to go too deep too soon.

Do make it clear when the interview has finished, and thank the interviewee for all that has been shared with you. I have memories of being interviewed and, just as the interviewers concluded the interview the tea and biscuits arrived. They very kindly offered some to me, and then began to ask me more questions. It was rather unnerving, but finishing a mouthful of biscuit does present you with an opportunity to think more before answering a question.

Attitudes to prayer at the beginning or end of the interview will vary according to the perspective of the interviewer and interviewee. At one level, I would argue that any deep, honest and open sharing of spiritual things is happening in God's presence and might be considered as prayer; for others a specific prayer will be important. The most important thing is to be true to yourself and to God. It is not helpful to create an environment where candidates feel that they need to pray and they then pray because of this pressure, rather than because they want to. Neither is it helpful to try to put your own conclusions about the interview into God's mind. If prayer is used manipulatively then it is blasphemous.

Some might find that a short period of silence at the end of the interview allows both interviewer and interviewee to commit the interview to God in prayer, without the need for spoken words. If you are doing this, do clearly indicate what is happening since you will not want the interviewee to be struggling with an unexplained silence at the end of the interview.

Part 4

INTERVIEWING

10

What about me?

Reflect . . .

What examples have you had of feeling uneasy or emotionally or spiritually threatened within an interview?

The questions that I ask in an interview might be threatening and challenging to the people that I interview, but framing my questions and hearing their answers can also be threatening and challenging to me. Also, I often need to take stock and question what right I have to sit in judgement upon another person.

I need to keep constantly aware of the fact that I am a fallen person with my own share of failure and unachieved aspirations; with hurts and losses that have been only partly dealt with. Sometimes I can notice my scar tissue or realize that there is still tenderness and vulnerability. Of course, it is because I am not perfect, and I can understand that others are not perfect, that I can dare to ask certain questions. It is because I have experienced pain and rejection that I know what this feels like and can begin to imagine what the candidate might feel like, so that I can sensitively try to explore this.

Although most of my hurts have been self-inflicted, there were other people who helped trigger the events and I will come across candidates who, for different reasons, remind me of them and remind me that I am still tender and vulnerable. Because I might be wary of such people there is a risk that I will project some of my feelings on to the candidate.

If I interview someone who has had episodes within his or her life that are quite similar to some of the episodes within mine, or someone who looks at the world in a similar way to me and shares similar aspirations and pain, there is a danger that I will over-empathize with that person.

My Christian faith is deeply important to me and shapes my views and opinions. I hold strong views about certain issues where others might see complexities and ambiguities, or I might see ambiguities and complexities where others hold clear-cut views. For example, I am grateful for my Christian upbringing and that I was baptized by sprinkling as a baby. I will, however, interview people who were baptized by immersion as adults who, through their answers about God's grace in their lives, might imply that my baptism was not valid.

There will be people whose walk with the Lord is so clear, and whose faith is so strong, that I will end up questioning the validity of my own discipleship and questioning whether I really have the depth of faith that God expects of me. There will be others whose assumptions and understandings will strike me as naïve and out of touch with the real world, but this might make me wonder if the same accusations could be made about some aspects of my own faith.

Bias and prejudice

At times we will all be aware of bias and prejudice. If we are not aware of it, then we should be particularly wary: it is still likely to be happening and our lack of awareness means it will be far harder to remedy!

Prejudice means to pre-judge. It means that we have begun to make assumptions about someone, and begun to make up our mind about that person before we have the evidence to do so. We normally assume that prejudice is a negative judgement about someone; it can equally be a positive judgement. If we are not prepared to ask the searching questions about aspects of someone's life, because we have already come to a positive conclusion, we will not be doing that person justice nor will we be doing justice to the processes that we are part of. Positive prejudice is just as bad and just as dangerous as negative prejudice.

We can have biases or prejudices about people for various reasons.

Sex

Some people may have had experiences with the opposite sex that leads them to make assumptions about them. Certain areas of ministry have, traditionally, been male only so there can easily be prejudice either against or in favour of women exploring that ministry.

Ethnicity

As a result of our previous contact (or lack of previous contact) with different ethnic groups we can easily make assumptions. If we have rarely come across someone from a particular ethnic group within a particular ministry then there can easily be an assumption either that it is not the right ministry for such a person, or that we should be overcoming barriers to make sure that the person is accepted.

Names

Last names might suggest that people come from a particular place; to the English person, some names sound particularly Welsh, Irish, Scottish, European or American. Other names might suggest a particular religious background: Roman Catholic, Jewish, Islamic, Sikh or Hindu. Certain names can suggest a particular social standing. First names, as well as doing the above can, particularly when associated with a person's age and what was going on in popular culture around the time of birth, suggest that the parents watched particular television programmes, followed certain pop stars or even supported a particular sports team.

Education and profession

The paperwork will tell us about the type of education that a person had and the work that he or she has gone on to do. Depending upon our own education and the people that we have met who have had a different education from us, we may make assumptions based upon educational background. There are also certain jobs that we cannot imagine ourselves doing, possibly for moral or ethical reasons, possibly because of the skills or temperament required. Again we can make assumptions.

Experiences or lifestyle

There are certain experiences or lifestyles that we are aware that we would not want to experience. There might be some issues that, of themselves, we do not disapprove of, but we might know others who have started with similar experiences or lifestyles and these have led them down a path that we strongly disapprove of. Again, it will be easy for us to make assumptions.

Christian vocabulary

All of us have our own Christian vocabulary and can easily find that certain Christian words or phrases can trigger reactions within us, perhaps reminding us of others who have used such terms.

Making assumptions

Making assumptions from the paperwork can be a good thing, as long as you remember that they are only assumptions and that they need exploration. Assumptions become dangerous only if they lead us on to become biased about the person. You will already be aware of the candidate's name, education, profession, sex and possibly ethnicity before the interview, and this allows you more time to identify any assumptions and to be aware of any prejudices.

It's more difficult to be aware of prejudices that might develop once an interview has started. The candidate might say something that means you pigeon-hole him or her as a particular 'type' of person; for example, mention of a favourite television programme or football team may lead you to jump to all sorts of conclusions.

Real life . . .

An interviewee mentioned the newspaper she read and felt the interview immediately went downhill from there. The interviewer assumed all sorts of things about her politics and her level of education without making any attempt to gain evidence to justify these assumptions.

There will also be people who, in some way, remind us of someone else: perhaps someone who has had power or influence over us; or someone who has caused us hurt or stood in the way of our aspirations; or a person who has shown prejudice against us, because of our agenda or our looks or our views; or someone who we have not liked or have been afraid of in the past. I remember one interviewer commenting that an interviewee reminded her of her ex-husband and this brought out all sorts of feelings and prejudice within her and she felt that any conclusions from her interview were likely to be invalid. Such feelings might be triggered by appearance, scent or after-shave, or accent or mannerisms as well as the experiences or the lifestyle or vocabulary issues mentioned above.

What can you do about prejudice?

Reflect . . .

Can you recognize if you have positive or negative prejudices about a candidate? Are there signs that you can look for?

If you are going to be able to do anything about your prejudices – and we all have them – then first of all you need to be able to recognize that they affect you. The warning signs may be different for each of us: often it will, literally, be a gut feeling – a sensation in your stomach; it might be a feeling of anger, confusion or empathy; you might become aware of a more aggressive style of reasoning or of being more dismissive of other views and positions; it might be a tensing of the muscles, or an increase in your heart rate, or a change in your body language.

Before the interview

Recognizing prejudice before an interview gives you an opportunity to try to deal with it and defuse it. In extreme cases, you may wish to avoid that particular interview and see if it is possible for someone else to conduct the interview in your place.

If you acknowledge your prejudice to someone else before the interview then the very act of bringing it out into the open and discussing it can help you to deal with it. Committing the issue to prayer can be a way of letting the Holy Spirit work upon your feelings.

You can also try to structure the interview so that you try to find a neutral area to begin with, rather than immediately getting into the areas where you know that your prejudices are working.

I have memories of interviewing a couple who had sent me a glossy testimony about the vision that lay behind their calling. Everything about the way in which it was written and its vocabulary sounded simplistic and brought out the worst in me. Had I started by asking them to tell me about their calling I am sure I would have fed my prejudices and confirmed my bias. Instead, I asked them to begin at the beginning, and take me through their lives. As I listened to the story of God's grace at work, particularly in the husband's life and in the healing, not only of physical illness, but also of relationships, I began to realize that if God had dealt so powerfully with such issues through the candidates' lives then that same God not only could, but would, speak as powerfully about vocation for this particular couple. By the time they began to describe the events leading to their sense of calling, it sounded the most natural way for God to be working within their lives.

During the interview

Dealing with prejudice that arises during an interview is harder. Once you have identified that it is happening, you need to try to isolate your feelings and distinguish your prejudices from your intuition. Remind yourself that you are seeking evidence to justify, or contradict, any feelings that you have. Your prejudice might leave you feeling negative about a particular area or issue that you have explored and you must not allow this to be carried over into other parts of the interview. Approach each issue with an open mind and seek the evidence to make objective decisions.

After the interview

Sometimes you will become aware of your prejudice only when you are reflecting on how the interview went and evaluating your conclusions. After the interview, acknowledge any prejudice that you were aware of before, during or after the interview. This should be mentioned in your reports and when you pass on comments and conclusions to others involved within the selection process.

Learning from your prejudices

It is not a pleasant experience to realize that you have prejudices. As mentioned, often the trigger of the prejudice will be linked with previous experiences that hurt or embarrassed you and you would much rather let go of these and bury them deeply in the past. Discovering your feelings might be the opportunity to deal more fully with whatever the problem was.

What threatens us?

Although I have focused on how your own experiences can lead you to be prejudiced during an interview, there can be other occasions when you are hurt or threatened but your judgement is not clouded by prejudice. This can still have an impact upon the interview.

You might find that suddenly being in touch with your own hurts and failures means that you are reluctant to explore fully someone else's in case this sets off your own pain. If this is the case, you will not do justice to the exploration of the issues that you are meant to be covering.

You might find that your own judgement and understanding is clouded and distorted by your own experiences. I have been aware of exploring another person's grief and loss at times when I have still been working through my own grief and their answers have been swamped by my own feelings, so I have not done justice to their answers. Going through such feelings is a natural part of the grieving process, but if they go on longer than they should then there is an issue that needs to be dealt with.

Through interviewing, you may become aware that there are issues that you do still need to deal with and to pray about and reflect upon in front of God. When I interviewed a counsellor she explained that for every ten hours of counselling she would receive one hour of supervision, so that she could unburden herself of what she was listening to and the impact that it was making upon her. You might not want to go as far as setting up such a system, but it is helpful to find a colleague, friend, mentor or spiritual director with whom you can share some of your feelings and with whom you can talk openly about the way that your interviewing interacts with your own faith and about the questions and struggles that you face as a result of your interviewing. In doing so, you will want to be aware of the confidential nature of the material that comes from your interviews. You will need to make sure that anything you say does not break a candidate's confidence by indicating who that candidate is. Of course, it is also possible that the interviewing process could raise issues that require you to seek professional help.

In-depth interviewing can certainly bring us deeply in touch with ourselves and our vulnerabilities and this is not always a pleasant experience. It is when we realize that there are unresolved issues that, with God's grace, we can begin to deal with them. Interviewing to test Christian vocation is a way of enabling other people to reach their full potential; one of its greatest rewards is that it can also help to bring us to our own full potential.

11

Using your eyes

Reflect . . .

What do you expect to get from the paperwork before an interview?

Reading the paperwork

Only by reading the paperwork thoroughly can you make a decision about whether or not to take candidates any further in the process. It is a waste of everybody's time, and very offensive to the candidates, to invite them for an interview and then to turn them down for a reason that was perfectly clear from the paperwork. They will assume that the paperwork was read properly and that the real reason you are turning them down has emerged at the interview and is now being hidden from them. (For more about how to ensure your paperwork is effective see Chapter 7.)

In some instances, having read the paperwork, you might find it appropriate to have a 'vocational chat'. If so, make sure that you have clearly indicated that this is what is on offer rather than letting the candidate think that he or she is beginning to go through a process that is testing vocation.

In order to interview well you need to prepare well. This means carefully reading any paperwork and preparing before the interview. The interviewee will have spent time and effort completing the paperwork and if you respect this you will do justice to what has been presented. The interviewee's confidence in the process will be undermined if you are repeatedly asking for information that should be obvious from the paperwork.

The amount of time needed for preparation will depend upon the stage within the process, and how much paperwork there is. At the final interview stage you may need an hour or more to work through the paperwork for each candidate and identify the issues that need to be explored at final selection. It is certainly not appropriate to hand out the paperwork when the interviewers arrive, allowing minimal time for preparation.

It is almost impossible to conduct a good interview without having something on paper about the candidate first; a CV is helpful, but it is best to work with standard paperwork with which you are familiar so that you know what you are looking for and where to find it. In the case of a non-competitive process there's no harm in supplementing this with a CV.

Reading systematically

Increasingly, the paperwork you receive will be word-processed. This means that you will no longer need to struggle with illegible writing or with trying to photocopy something that is too faint to copy properly. Given that word-processing packages have spelling and grammar checks, the days of making judgements about someone on the basis of spelling and handwriting are very much over, and the more obvious grammatical mistakes have also mainly vanished from applications.

If you are testing the vocation of both husband and wife, then it is worth trying to tell, perhaps from the language and style of writing, if they have each completed their own form. If one person seems to have completed both, this could suggest that the vocation belongs to one and that the other is a passive partner. Of course, there may be a very different explanation: one partner may have been away when the forms were completed or one may be uncomfortable using a word processor.

As is made clear in Chapter 13, exploring times of change during the interview process can provide a rich source of material about how people make decisions and how they adjust to different situations. The key to finding when such events have occurred is within the paperwork.

It is helpful to build up a chronological picture of events within the candidates' life. Where were they born? Where did they go to school? Did they have a stable family life? Did they move house a lot during childhood? Were such moves at times that might have proved difficult within their education? Did they go through the different stages of education at the usual ages? When were different courses studied, and did they follow on naturally from each other or do they indicate changes of direction professionally? When did any job changes occur? Are there any patterns to the frequency of job changes? Are there any years unaccounted for?

It's always worth exploring gaps. There's a very entertaining film on interviewing produced by the Industrial Society in which the comedian John Cleese shows how not to conduct a good interview, and in one instance he fails to explore the gap in the CV when the candidate was actually in prison!

Dates in a CV or on an application form can be revealing. For instance, if there were long periods without or between children, was this deliberate or was this a time of despair or of grieving for repeated miscarriages? Was a child born seven years after the previous one planned and welcomed or an unexpected arrival that was only grudgingly accepted into the family? Why did someone spend only three months in a job? Was it because the employer asked the person to leave during the probationary period, or did the candidate leave of his or her own accord, and why?

It is also worth remembering that it is quite easy for a candidate to get the odd date wrong. You might go in to an interview keen to explore something that looks interesting because of the dates, only to find that there hadn't been a year's unemployment or that a child hadn't been born two years before marriage; instead there is just a mistake with a date.

Increasingly, CVs are being written thematically, rather than chronologically. In this way, candidates offers prospective employers the picture that they wish to offer of who they are and what skill, qualifications and expertise they offer. It is helpful to have this picture of how they wish to present themselves, but it is also important to find out how the person became like this. You could make a note of their education and jobs in chronological order so that you can build up a picture of how the person progressed to who he or she is now.

Reading deeply

As well as approaching the paperwork systematically, you may like to mull over it 'prayerfully'. Without wanting to over-spiritualize, it is helpful to offer the person and the process to God and invite the Holy Spirit to help to make any connections that are in the paperwork, perhaps noticing patterns or inconsistencies in behaviour in different episodes of the person's life that have been recounted.

It is in mulling over the papers that you are able to notice patterns, or particular use of certain words or phrases, within the answers. For example, is God always referred to as God, Jesus, Father or Holy Spirit? If you are interviewing couples then it can be interesting to see whether they are using the same words and phrases and giving identical or similar answers.

Making a plan

At whatever stage in the process you are conducting an interview, after adequate preparation, you should know what issues you want to explore. It is helpful to write down a list of headings, in an approximate order, to remind you of the main issues that you wish to cover during the interview.

Once you have read all the paperwork systematically and mulled it over you may find it helpful to make a plan of the interview and the areas that you intend to cover. If it is a first interview then anything you discover is new information and you may not need a very specific plan, although you will probably have noted some issues that need exploration.

If it is not an initial interview, then you will need to identify very specific issues for follow-up. These will be issues that have not already been fully considered and that earlier interviews suggest would be worth covering. In these cases read through all the existing paperwork and interview reports and write down the issues that should be explored. When you have a list, work out the best order to approach the issues in: the interview should have a direction so that you are not just jumping around randomly. (For good questions to start an interview with, see p. 133.)

Having made a plan, don't be too tied to it. A word or comment may mean that it is more natural to move to some other topic on the list and then go back to the next issue. Also, an issue may emerge that is not on your plan at all, but that still needs investigation.

At final selection there should be a very clear brief of what issues need further exploration and each interviewer should know exactly which issues to examine with each candidate and will go into the interview with a checklist of topics.

Gaining perspective

When you read paperwork before deciding whether to invite someone for interview, then you are using your eyes to make judgements about that person. During the interview your eyes should not be used to make a judgement, but they can and should be used to add a different perspective and to help you decide additional areas that need to be explored.

Increasingly, organizations conduct an initial interview (or a pre-interview) over the phone. I have never tried to do this and would feel totally inadequate in doing so because I would be deprived of the perspective that my eyes bring.

First impressions

Reflect . . .

What sort of impression might you begin to gain about a candidate in the first five minutes of meeting with them?
How much of this is based on what you see rather than what you hear?

First impressions are, of course, just that, and they are not and should not be final impressions. Remember that the interview situation can be intimidating and the candidate may be very nervous. Additionally, sometimes people will have travelled far and set off very early and may not be presenting themselves as well as they might wish.

Consider whether or not first impressions are important for the role that you are interviewing for. In some types of ministry people will need to be able to make a very positive impact or their first contact might end up being their only contact; in many other ministries this is not so important.

First impressions can determine how much you warm to a person and, of course, warming to a person can be a very dangerous thing as it might mean that you only explore the positive and avoid the negative aspects that might get in the way of your positive impression.

First impressions may also highlight issues that need to be explored either at this interview or at a subsequent interview. You need to be aware of this first visual impact and consider whether you are empathizing or feeling uncomfortable. Try to ask yourself if your response is shaping or changing the interview in any way.

If the person is nervous, see if you can encourage him or her to feel more relaxed. If self-confidence seems to be lacking, then this may well be an issue you need to explore; equally, overconfidence will need looking at.

I find myself surprised that I am not commenting here about how people dress. I am sure that within competitive interviews this still has some importance but in the non-competitive vocational-type interview there will be huge diversity between formal and informal clothing, although candidates will still want to present themselves in a way that suggests that they are taking the process seriously.

Making observations

Reflect . . .

As the interview progresses, what can you see that might affect your view of a candidate?

As we spend longer with someone, we can make observations about the person that might lead us to pursue particular issues. Some examples from my own experience follow here.

- If smoking will cause a barrier to the ministry, it can be helpful to explore whether the yellow stain on certain fingers is nicotine or whether the candidate has just repainted the bathroom in a rather dull yellow. (With this particular issue, using your nose can be helpful as well!)
- Scars on the wrist might be the result of an unfortunate encounter with a thorn bush or might be the result of an unsuccessful suicide attempt. It is going to be important to find out and not make assumptions.

> **Real life . . .**
>
> The interviewer eventually noticed the scars on the candidate's left wrist when her cardigan rode slightly up her arm. Noticing the way that she used her hands, he judged that she was right-handed. Later in the interview, when they had developed a greater rapport, he did ask the question of how she had gained the scars and heard about her two suicide attempts.

- Extreme slimness can be the result of anorexia. It is very difficult to get someone who is currently anorexic to admit it, but often there are pointers to it in other aspects of the person's life, particularly in other obsessive behaviour and in the relationship with the parents. Other obsessive behaviour – for example a compulsive attitude to sport or exercise – may also replace anorexia. It is an area that is best left to the professionals to explore and draw conclusions from.

- Sometimes observation can lead us to think that we are aware of someone's sexuality, and I mean 'sexuality' in its broadest sense of how people do, or don't, express their sexual identity and whether they appear to be comfortable with who they are. If you feel that what is being hinted at with regard to sexuality or sexual identity might not be appropriate in certain contexts, then this will be something you may feel you should ask about.

- Tattoos, body piercing, hair length and wigs might all be saying something about a person, tattoos and certain body piercings being rather permanent statements. If they are saying something, it is important to ask and find out what they are saying rather than jump to conclusions.

Body language

You might notice that a question, or a particular line of questioning, produces a physical response in the interviewee. Again, it should be stressed that what you see gives you a perspective, rather than conclusions, but the perspective that you gain might lead you to look into certain issues more deeply.

- Control: the 'steepling' movement of the hands and fingers, with fingers pointing up and fingertips touching or fingers interlocked, usually indicates that the person feels that they are in control. Given that you should be controlling the interview, observing this action in a candidate indicates that you probably need to take some initiative to regain control of the interview.
- Evaluation: the use of the hand to stroke the face or hair, either directly or by using perhaps glasses or a pen usually indicates that someone is reflecting and evaluating information. It can be helpful to observe this going on, and you probably won't want to interrupt the process but you may see it as an opportunity to explore further the issue that has prompted such reflection.
- Defence: your questions might make the interviewee feel defensive. Sometimes the interviewee might literally be feeling 'hot under the collar' and be running a finger between their collar and neck. More often, a physical barrier might appear, such as interlocked hands or folded arms. The barrier may also be made by the candidate suddenly crossing the legs, perhaps even just at the ankles. We do need to remember that candidates will sit in different ways because that is how they are comfortable and that it is sudden changes in response to questions that should interest us. It can be helpful to know if someone is becoming defensive, but judgement is needed to know what to do with the knowledge. On one occasion I was exploring the bereavement of a widow and became aware that there was a deep defensiveness, which I felt sure I needed to explore further. When I asked what the husband had died from, I got the details of his suicide; I felt the need to explore why he had taken his own life and found out that the wife had threatened to leave him the previous day! It was important that I found this out, but we won't always want to hear what can come out when someone is being defensive, nor know what to make of it.
- Openness: the opposite side of the coin is openness, which can be indicated by opening up the body, or the legs. If this follows after barriers have been put up, it can indicate that the defensive phase has passed.
- Nervousness: interviewees can play with their hair or their jewellery and do things with their fingers that look positively painful. These types of activity generally indicate worry or nervousness

and might indicate that there is something that we need to investigate further. Some organizations helpfully provide visitors with a security badge, just in case they have not brought anything of their own to fiddle with! Covering of mouth can be a sign of embarrassment.

- Sudden changes: of particular interest is any sudden change of body language that appears to be triggered by a particular question, or even by a response to your question.

Interviewing couples

When interviewing a couple try to sit them in a way that allows you to observe them both. As well as observing the body language of the one who is answering, it can be interesting to cast an occasional glance at the other one. You may observe boredom with hearing a well-known story or fascination in hearing an episode that has never been heard before. There can also be times when the partner who is not speaking can show deep embarrassment at the answer that is being given. The body language between the couple may express something of the dynamics that is going on between them during the interview – sometimes moments of loving support and affirmation and sometimes not!

Your own body language

It is interesting to watch someone else's body language and try to draw conclusions from it but it is important to be aware of your own body language too. The interviewee might have a deeper understanding of what body language means than you do! It can be valuable to observe your own body language occasionally, and to try to identify what it might be saying and whether you are comfortable with the vibes that you are giving out.

If you are trying to explore something that you might not feel comfortable with, are you giving out all of the vibes of someone who is nervous? When we suddenly find the well-hidden vulnerability, and begin to explore it sensitively, are we looking as if we are empathizing, or are we 'steepling' away like mad because at last we feel that we are in control of the interview?

A very helpful exercise is to be videoed carrying out a role-play interview and to watch the re-run of the video. Body language will also occur, in-role, when we role-play; it can be an interesting and enlightening experience. I hadn't realized how much I used my hands to gesture with, until I first watched myself on video. The second time I went into it prepared, I virtually sat on my hands, keeping them rigidly by my side. This had the effect of me gesturing with my head instead of my hands. I concluded that I preferred to watch the hand gestures!

Interaction of body languages

Our body languages can interact with each other; there can be a tendency to mirror the body language that we are observing. I have been aware of interviewees who were not looking relaxed and were perched on the front of their chair. I found that by copying their position for a few minutes, and then moving to a more relaxed position, I managed to encourage them to move to a more comfortable position as well.

Body language can be a helpful tool, but you do need to remember that people do periodically move their limbs in order to keep comfortable; they scratch because they have an itch and cover their mouths because they are going to cough or yawn. Anything that you see within an interview can give you clues as to what you need to explore further but it cannot in itself lead you to draw conclusions. It's also worth noting that while some body language is probably universal, some might vary from culture to culture.

12

Using your ears

There is a reason that God gave us two ears and only one mouth: he expects us to listen much more than we talk. This is particularly true of interviewing. The purpose of the interview is to get the interviewee to speak. To do this we need to ask certain questions, but the more time that we spend speaking, the less the interviewee can speak.

Real life . . .

Every time an interviewee gave a significant answer the interviewer gave a long reply affirming the wisdom of the answer. Although the interviewee felt affirmed he also felt constrained. He had not been allowed to share of himself as much as he should and therefore hadn't done himself justice.

Although the interviewer may have affirmed his selection, there really wasn't much evidence on which to base this decision.

You may find that a candidate shows an interest in who you are and what you think about certain issues. It is reassuring to find this pastoral concern from the interviewee, but the interview is not the place to answer these questions. Tell the interviewee that you are grateful for the interest but that you don't want to take up interview time by talking about yourself and you'd be happy to talk to him or her outside of the interview process.

Barriers to effective listening

Reflect . . .

What kind of things can stop you listening to someone properly?

Find out what it feels like to speak to people who are responding to you in different ways by working with someone who will spend ten minutes with you exploring the following exercises.

- Stand back-to-back, so that you cannot see each other at all, and take it in turns to speak for a couple of minutes about a pre-chosen topic.
- Face each other and spend a couple of minutes both speaking, on a pre-chosen topic, at the same time.
- Face each other and take it in turns to speak for a couple of minutes about a pre-chosen topic but the one who is listening must not speak or make any grunts or sounds, must not keep eye contact and must not give any other form of affirmation.

Discuss together how these experiences feel.

When interviewing you need to be an 'active' listener. It is very difficult for people to keep talking for even two minutes if they feel that they are getting no reaction to what they are saying. In the normal course of conversation, even if we are not speaking, we will make little noises and grunts, at appropriate places, to indicate that we are following what is being said. We will also use our facial expression to affirm the other person as he or she speaks and to show that we are listening and interested in what is being said.

An absence of these affirmations indicates that you are not listening or interested. If you are going to encourage the interviewee to speak and to share openly you will need to be continually showing affirmation and encouragement. You should be particularly aware when such affirmation and encouragement is especially needed. The interviewee is unlikely to tell you to your face that you are not listening; instead he or she will just stop speaking or stop sharing at the deeper level that you are hoping for.

Just as it can be helpful to video a role-play to observe your body language it can also be a helpful exercise for showing how well you listen. Try to do this with someone else involved in interviewing and take turns to be the interviewer. You can then honestly (and lovingly) point out each other's strengths and weaknesses. It can be very revealing to observe the occasions where it appears that your concentration and your listening is not 100 per cent and the impact that this has upon the interviewee.

One of the dilemmas with interviewing is that, as well as listening, you need to be directing the interview. This means reflecting upon what has been said, thinking about what else needs exploring and deciding the best way to do so. Consider when to move from one topic to another and how to do this as seamlessly as possible. If you cannot do this without indicating a lapse in concentration, it will be worth having the occasional silence. Don't be afraid of silences, or of saying 'just a moment while I remember what I was going to ask next'.

Another barrier can be paperwork. A quick glance at your papers to confirm a detail is usually all right, but if it looks as if you are intently reading the paperwork, it will suggest that you are no longer listening properly. Again, asking the interviewee to stop for a moment while you check a detail will be more reassuring than giving the impression that you are more interested in the paperwork than in the interviewee as a person.

You may need to take some notes during the interview (see Chapter 15), but if the interviewee suddenly gets the idea that you are writing an essay, a letter or a shopping list, rather than listening, they are likely to dry up.

What isn't said?

As well as being aware of what is being said, you can also, as an interview develops, get an idea of what isn't being said. You might want to return to an issue or episode and ask more specific questions to encourage a deeper sharing. Alternatively, you might feel that it is difficult to explore these areas without specific preparation and therefore note them afterwards as issues that should be discussed at a subsequent interview. Being warned about trickier issues for exploration gives an opportunity to reflect upon different ways of getting into these issues.

Well-rehearsed narratives

Sometimes you may get the feeling that an answer is delivered so smoothly that it has obviously been well rehearsed. This may be because the candidate has prepared very thoroughly for the inter-view or because he or she is used to sharing the story in their work. Yet the fact that a narrative is well rehearsed does not mean that it is the only possible interpretation of events. In such cases make sure that you are ask questions that allow other interpretations and other people's perspectives of events to be reflected upon.

Clarifying what you have heard

Given that interviewees will not always be very clear, that stories and episodes can be confusing and that the telling of them can also be confusing, it is well worth clarifying that what you have heard is what has really been said. The interviewee should be reassured by the fact that you are concerned to clarify what has been said and are not prepared to live with any doubt or ambiguity that you have.

13

Using your lips

As suggested in Chapter 9, each interview will have a different task depending upon where in the selection and interview process it is coming.

Digging deeper

I find it helpful to consider a person as resembling an onion that is made up of the layers that are shown in the figure here.

On the surface are facts; facts are verifiable and will include the information provided on a CV. Just below this layer are thoughts; these are the views that we readily give and they reflect how we choose to portray ourselves. Beneath this layer is behaviour; all of us are aware to a large extent of how we act, but others may have a different understanding of our behaviour. Beneath this layer we find attitudes and assumptions; these will shape our behaviour and,

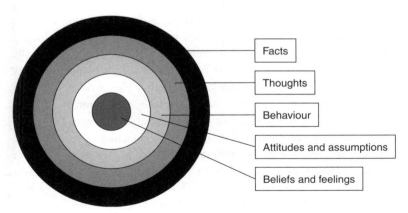

Onion layer model

in turn, flow from the beliefs and feelings positioned at the centre of the onion. Both beliefs and feelings can often be hard to find out about and you might need to probe quite deeply to discover what is really there.

I have mentioned both thoughts and beliefs and put beliefs at the heart of the onion. It can be easy to hear someone's thoughts but to think that you have heard their beliefs. Beliefs should lead to lifestyle and action, and these might be quite different from what a person thinks that they should do, or thinks that you want to hear. For example, a question that relates faith, stewardship and the poor begs a particular answer and might well stimulate an answer that is the result of thinking, rather than reflect the beliefs that will actually lead to behaviour.

Obviously, when selecting from among Christians, you expect to find Christianity at the centre of their beliefs, but there will also be cultural norms present. Different understandings of the gospel will be deeply conditioned by culture, and often it is only when a probing question is asked that someone will begin to become aware of what their beliefs really are. This is why I have positioned beliefs, together with feelings, at the heart of the onion.

When people are asked about how they felt about something, they might well answer, 'I felt that . . .' But in reality they may be telling you about their thoughts, and not their feelings.

Try to fashion the interview questions so that you gradually probe more deeply by peeling away the layers of the onion – initially finding out facts and thoughts and then behaviour, but then getting beneath these to discover the attitudes and assumptions and the feelings and beliefs at the core. If you try to go straight to the heart of the onion and to explore beliefs and feelings you won't really know if the answers obtained are authentic. It is only by peeling away these outer layers that you will know whether the answers obtained at the core are consistent with their attitudes and assumptions.

The main task in interviewing is to find out about facts, thoughts, behaviour, attitudes, assumptions, beliefs and feelings – information that the interviewee knows about himself or herself that we don't yet know. Some of the clues as to how others perceive the candidate's behaviour, attitudes, assumptions, beliefs and feelings will be obtained from the assumptions of the referees, who know the candidate, or from the home church.

How deep should you go?

The depth of exploration will depend upon the purpose underlying the processes. You will certainly need to probe issues deeply enough to determine whether you are accepting the candidate, but if you also wish to give pastoral and spiritual support to help the candidate reach his or her full potential in Christ, you may need to go even further. If you have sent out preliminary information about the interview process and its purpose and have explained the need for thorough exploration of issues (see Chapter 7), candidates should have come prepared to share deeply of themselves.

Real life . . .

An interviewer was trying to explore a candidate's broken engagement, though she really didn't want to discuss this episode of her life. Yet the interviewer felt it was right to persist with this line of questioning: it appeared that the candidate had so many unresolved issues about this matter that it wasn't right for the application to proceed further at this time. The interviewer couldn't have come to this conclusion if she hadn't persisted with her line of questioning.

Interview questions

Interviews should involve asking a range of different types of question in order to elicit different types or levels of information. When doing this you will need to observe the interviewee's style and method of response, clarify issues as you go, and keep the discussion relevant.

Getting started

There is probably no such thing as a 'safe' question. Sometimes candidates are aware that there is something very significant in their life and have concluded that they want to share this story, and will want to get on with it and unburden themselves early on. I have interviewed people when I have known from the paperwork, or what they have told me on the phone or by letter or email, that the last job didn't work out. In such cases it can be worth exploring that issue first. Such candidates know that they need to talk about it and have probably worked out what they want to say; they are unlikely to do justice to other questions until they think that they have unburdened themselves about that particular episode.

Real life . . .

An interviewer wished to make polite conversation when he met an interviewee at reception. He asked what had made the young man decide to live in the town he has just travelled from. The answer given was that a judge had issued a court order that he live at least 100 miles away from a certain young woman!

There were various ways in which the interviewee could have answered this question; the judge had still left him with plenty of other towns where he could live and he had obviously made decisions in narrowing down his options and choosing that particular place. If he had given a different, but still truthful, answer the interviewer would not have been any wiser (although it is to be hoped that, during the course of the interview, issues about how the interviewee related to women would have come out).

It might well be that you give a candidate the opportunity to speak about such an episode early within the interview, and ask one or two questions for clarity, and then return to the episode later in the interview when, with the understanding that you have gained of the candidate, you will have a better idea of the specific issues that you wish to explore. As mentioned in Chapter 12, such events often produce a well-rehearsed narrative. It is good to reflect on such a narrative and then return to it to ask questions that can take you deeper into what was really happening.

Occasionally you may be told very deep and intimate information early on within an interview, but normally it is best to create an atmosphere and a relationship that allows this to happen in time.

If you are conducting an initial interview and beginning the process of finding out information about the candidate, consider opening the interview by either asking the candidate to 'tell me about why you have come here today' or to 'tell me about the family that you were born into'. Both are very good ways to begin and allow the interviewee to provide narrative and facts, so that you can choose areas to explore more deeply. Asking the question 'tell me about why you have come here today' deliberately avoids putting any spiritual or vocational vocabulary into the question and allows the candidate to choose to respond with his or her own vocabulary. The question will allow you to explore the factors that have influenced the sense of vocation; these will often originate many years in the past or will have been influenced by circumstances that occurred in childhood. At this point you could switch to the 'family' question and encourage the candidate to tell you his or her story leading up to the here and now.

Narrative questions ('Tell me about . . .') provide a good and usually safe start to the interview. They allow candidates to feel relaxed and confident and not to feel the need to be defensive or that someone is trying to catch them out. Sometimes candidates might tell you all sorts of things about themselves without any further prompting, but always there will be a need to direct the conversation and take it into the direction that you want to explore rather than allowing them to make all the running. The time that you have available, and the material that you need to cover, will determine how much you will need to control the interview.

Closed questions

Reflect . . .

Do you know the difference between an open question and a closed question? Which type of question was that?

Questions that can produce very limited answers are described as closed questions. So, for example, the question, 'Do you know the difference between an open question and a closed question?' is a closed question because there are only two possible answers: 'yes' or 'no'. Similarly, 'Which type of question was that?' is also a closed question because it can only be answered from a previously offered list of choices: 'open' or 'closed'. Such questions close down the conversation, rather than opening it up.

The type of answer that a question will produce is likely to be determined by the first word used in the question. The following will lead you to ask a closed question which results in a 'yes' or 'no' answer:

- do/did/does?
- can/could?
- will/would?
- shall/should?
- is/are?
- may/might?

Similarly, a question that begins with the word 'which' can only be answered by one of a set of pre-supplied answers.

Closed questions do have some uses. They can be helpful in clarifying the information that you have, for example for checking a date on a form. You may also want to sum up the information that you have heard and clarify that you have come to the correct conclusions. Don't be afraid to check in this way; it gives the candidate confidence to know that you will check if you are uncertain. Closed questions are also a good way of concluding one area of questioning and moving on to another. Asking, 'You then moved to ..., didn't you?' indicates that you have finished hearing about a particular episode and wish to move on to another subject.

Open questions

In contrast to a closed question, an open question is a question that opens up, or develops, the conversation. A rhyme, written by Rudyard Kipling, gives the six words that will usually produce questions that will open up the conversation:

> I have six honest serving-men.
> They taught me all I know.
> Their names are Who and What and When
> And Why and Where and How.

Each of these six open-question words should provide information about a different aspect of an issue; some are likely to lead to purely factual information ('who', 'when', 'where' and 'what'), but the others ('why' and 'how') should give information about attitudes, insights, thoughts or feelings.

Be aware that if you ask, 'What did you feel?' the answer given may indeed be about feelings, but if the word 'that' is added ('I feel that . . .'), you have probably been given an answer that is about thoughts rather than feelings. Although 'where' is usually given a factual response ('Where were you when you met your partner?'), if you ask, 'Where was God?' in a particular situation it should provide an answer that tells you about beliefs rather than geography.

Probing questions

By listening to the narrative that comes out of the 'tell me about' question, you can identify areas that you feel are worth exploring more deeply. If you are trying to understand the candidate's thoughts ('What do you think about . . . ?') be careful not to include your own thoughts in the question. Obviously, the question 'I think it's important we work for peace in the Middle East; what do you think?' is only going to elicit one answer. The fewer of your own thoughts that you have shared, the less likely it is that your thoughts will influence the answer (for more on this see leading questions, p. 137). It is, however, worth reflecting on the answers to questions about thoughts to see if anything so far in the conversation might be influencing how a candidate answers such questions.

Using questions that begin with 'how' or 'why' will get you deeper into understanding what has been going on and the candidate's own understanding of events and his or her impact upon them. You can also probe more deeply by asking, 'How did you feel?' The question, 'Is there anything else?' can also encourage a candidate to move on to deeper information.

Extending questions

Sometimes the candidate needs to be encouraged to share more about events and a simple 'tell me more' will often be enough to encourage this. Sometimes your intuition will nudge you to explore an area further. Such intuition might be the result of the candidate's body language or use of language, or it may just be a feeling that you have.

If the interviewee answers your question with a generality or the answer is rather ambiguous, don't be afraid to ask, 'What are you thinking of specifically?' Not only can this clarify the answer but it can help you to avoid making false assumptions.

Don't be scared of pauses. Often a pause will be the stimulus that is needed for the candidate to continue with the narrative. Often, when trying to find the right question to encourage the candidate to tell me more, I find that before I can phrase my question or comment, he or she has resumed the answer and provided me with the deeper information I was seeking. Another way to extend the answer is to ask, 'What else could you have done?'

Comparative questions

Encouraging the candidate to make comparisons can be fruitful in different ways. It is possible to ask, 'How does this compare with that?' or, 'What has happened since then?' By comparing one situation with another, the candidate is showing not only an ability to reflect but is also making value judgements, and (as will be mentioned further in Chapter 14) it can be helpful to take the candidate's words and feed them back. If a church is being described as lively or dead, or as evangelical or charismatic or catholic, then the use of that word can be explored. If a job is being described as more difficult or as more fulfilling, then the reasons behind this can be discussed.

Linking questions

Linking questions can serve two purposes within the interview: one is to give continuity to the interview; the other is to explore patterns. A linking question can create a smooth logical flow to the interview; this will depend on your listening skills and your ability to paraphrase or summarize answers. Within the interview, you will want to use the candidate's content and material while still keeping to your agenda. The knack is to pick up on the response of the candidate to the last question or an earlier one, in order to move on to the next area that you wish to explore. 'You mentioned earlier that there was a lot of change at that time; tell me, how did you feel about that?' or, 'On the subject of . . . , what has been people's initial response to your plans?'

I once interviewed someone who told me why several different events in his life had not worked out as well as he had hoped. For each episode a satisfactory reason was given but I noticed there was a pattern: each time all of the blame was projected upon someone else and never on himself. Once I had made this link it was helpful to re-explore some of the earlier events – perhaps by going back to an earlier occurrence and asking if he would have handled the situation differently if it happened again, or by asking if he had learnt anything about himself from the event.

Often seeing such a pattern can be more obvious after the interview, when you write up your report, than it is at the time of the interview. In such cases, unless yours is the final one, it is worth asking someone else to explore this pattern at a subsequent interview.

Counterproductive questions

There are some questions that are likely to be counterproductive.

Leading questions

As mentioned above, you should avoid questions that imply the answer you want to hear. If you ask a candidate, 'Are you sure that God is calling you to this agency?' you're unlikely to hear the answer, 'No, I'm not sure.' It would be better, having discussed the calling in a general way, to ask why the candidate felt that he or she was being called to your particular organization.

The question, 'You're pretty healthy, I assume?' implies that you want a positive answer, and you are therefore likely to get one. It would be better to explore generally someone's health record, including any significant times off work, and find out if any problems have been dealt with.

The question, 'It is very important that the person going to this job gets on well with young people. That's something you enjoy, no doubt?' is hardly likely to produce a negative answer. It would be better to ask what experience a candidate has working with young people and then see how enthusiastic he or she is about that work.

Multiple questions

Be careful not to fall into the trap of asking several questions in one go without leaving an opportunity for a response. The question,

'Would you mind the travel involved, and how would your family feel about it – although of course, they're probably used to it already, aren't they?' could, rightly, be answered with the reply 'I wouldn't mind; OK; no, not really.' Both interviewer and interviewee are likely to become confused!

Hypothetical questions

Hypothetical questions may be helpful when exploring how the interviewee reflects and reasons and engages with new concepts, but their role is limited. Within the onion model, a hypothetical question is about thoughts. It is far better to ask questions about behaviour by looking at previous experiences. If you are going to make a judgement about how someone deals with a particular situation, it is far better to find evidence of what the person has done in the past and what has been learnt from such experiences, than create a hypothetical situation in the future.

We will return to this when we consider exploring potential (see p. 140).

Exploring times of change

I find that some of the most helpful areas to explore in an interview are times of change. In fact, I find it very difficult to interview effectively those who have seldom needed to deal with times of change within their lives.

> **Reflect . . .**
>
> Recall a significant time of change within your own life. Perhaps you changed jobs, moved house or had children. Try and get in touch with the feelings you had at the time and imagine what you might say if an interviewer asked you about this time.

Think about what questions you might ask someone who moved jobs and, as a consequence, also moved home. You might start by saying, 'Tell me about your move to this new job.' What might you ask next? Here are some suggestions:

1 Why did you decide to change job?
2 How do you make decisions?
3 What different responsibilities did you have?
4 How did the new job feel?
5 What did you miss?
6 How did you choose your new church?
7 How did it compare with your old church?
8 What impact did this have upon your spiritual life?
9 How did this feel?
10 What have you done about this?
11 What did you learn as a result of this?
12 How did you choose where to live?
13 Did you have friends there?
14 How did you make new friends?
15 How long was it until you felt at home?
16 What effect did the move have on contact with your family?
17 What effect did it have on contact with friends?

Through these questions you would find out about a whole range of topics: job responsibilities, job satisfaction, decision-making, feelings about work, how the candidate chooses a church, value judgements about different types of churches, spiritual life, spiritual growth, feelings about spiritual life, choices about home, ability to adapt to different circumstances, ability to establish support networks, ability to sustain friendships, feelings about support systems.

Of course, you couldn't possibly ask all of these questions or make such a firm plan of questions before the interview, but you might discuss some of these points and the candidate's answers might raise a number of further issues that you would want to explore.

Times of change can coincide with times of vulnerability and growth. Asking, 'How have you changed?' or, 'What have you learnt?' not only tells you about growth and learning, it also lets the candidate know that you believe in growth and learning and that it is OK to share fragilities as well as strengths with you.

Asking what someone has learnt from an experience can be a good way of getting deeper answers. The question can, however, be answered in different ways. If someone has just narrated a rather negative episode in his or her life then the answer could be at three different levels: what was learnt about other people and about life;

what was learnt about self; what was learnt about God. I prefer to leave such a question general, and note which way the candidate chooses to answer it. If the initial answer is about what was learnt about other people then I can always come back to the question again and find out if anything was learnt anything about self or about God. If the candidate consistently learns only about other people and never about self or God, then I know I have another area to begin to explore. If the answers are just at the level of learning about God, I will still want to find out if there is any learning about self.

Working with the selection strategy window

Remind yourself of the selection strategy window on p. 49. This is a tool that can help you to think about the status of any information that you have and any conclusions that you are reaching: is the information knowledge or assumptions? Is the interviewee aware of the knowledge we have, or the assumptions we are likely to make? Remember, if we are to base our decisions or recommendations about training, suitable locations, and pastoral and spiritual support upon this information, it will be important that this information is knowledge that both we and the candidate are aware of.

Exploring potential

You will need to accept that you are unable to find the full potential of the candidate, but by exploring how the candidate has coped and functioned in the past you should be able to draw some conclusions. The candidate's potential is something that neither we nor the candidate really knows, so in making the connection between past experiences and their implication for how he or she might function in the future you will want not only to find out the answer for yourself, but to help the candidate discover the answer as well.

A particular temptation in exploring vocation to a ministry with which you are personally familiar is to think of some difficult situation that you have faced in the past then, after giving the interviewee only a few of the relevant facts, ask how he or she would respond and compare the response with yours. Not surprisingly, the interviewee usually comes up with a different answer. Again, don't ask hypothetical questions. Instead, ask questions about changes that the candidate has faced or ask about how the candidate has dealt with difficult relationships in the past. If you want to know how someone copes with disaster, ask about the worst thing that has ever happened to him or her. Such questions will give you some real material to assess; hypothetical scenarios tell you about reasoning and reflection.

Consistency

I mentioned earlier in this chapter that you can test what you find out about beliefs and feelings by checking if it is consistent with what you discover about attitudes, assumptions and behaviour (see p. 130). Similarly, by helping the candidate reflect more deeply on attitudes, assumptions and behaviour you can help him or her to discover and articulate beliefs and feelings. By encouraging articulation of these reflections, you will know that the candidate has made the self-discovery and shares a similar conclusion to yours. With some self-discovery there might be the need for 'space' before moving on in the exploration, either coming back to the issue later in the interview when both you and the candidate have reflected on what has emerged, or else agreeing to revisit the issue at a later date.

Summarizing your assumptions

Summarizing what you think you have heard is a good way of confirming that the interviewee is aware of how you are interpreting the information that you are getting. If, for example, the candidate has narrated a couple of episodes in which he or she has had difficulty in dealing with stress and none in which stress was readily dealt with, then by summarizing what you have heard you are not only moving your judgement (that stress is difficult for them) into the open, but also giving an opportunity for the candidate to provide examples that counter this judgement.

Previous interviews

If you are exploring the assumptions made by yourself or another interviewer, then the topic can be introduced by relating it to the previous conversation, whether this was with yourself or with a previous interviewer. Whether that original piece of information is leading you to draw positive or negative conclusions, you will want to explore other events in the candidate's life before feeling that you can draw definite conclusions.

Perhaps, for example, the candidate left home in 1999 for the first time and felt terribly homesick, and took ages to settle into a new job, a new home and a new church. It would be easy to draw negative conclusions from this. Three years later, in 2002, the candidate moved again and all went well that time. Is this just luck, or did the candidate learn from the experiences of 1999? You will need to explore further moves and so ask what happened during a further move in, say, 2005. The conclusions that we draw will come from putting together all this information. Why was there a different response at different times? What lessons were learnt from the initial experiences? Often you will find growth, but sometimes people lose confidence and abilities over the years and you cannot just assume that there will be growth; you need to find evidence.

Only when you have explored different issues at different stages in the candidate's life can you confidently feel that you know how he or she functions and, if you have reached a negative conclusion, feel confident that you have enough evidence to explain the reasons for your conclusion. You are unlikely to have all of the information but you should be able to feel confident that your conclusions are based on evidence rather than assumptions.

References

In exploring issues that come out of references, you need to ask yourself whether the candidate is likely to be aware of what the issues are. This, of course, involves all of the sensitivities mentioned above about helping candidates discover things about themselves that they were not previously aware of. It also has the potential for candidates to realize that others have made assumptions about them that they were not aware of, and have passed these assumptions on to you. These may be positive assumptions but, if not, this could be devastating.

If a referee or home church is providing you with new assumptions that are sensitive, then you will need to clarify whether the referee or church is prepared for you to reveal your source of information. You should not say anything that will damage the relationship between the referee or church and the candidate. Be aware that the candidate will know who has given references.

There are ways of sensitively examining assumptions without making the source of these obvious. If you have received comments about, for example, the quality of relationships that the candidate is able to develop and sustain, then you will want to carefully explore these relationships. You could generally discuss how the candidate has developed and sustained relationships in the past, the candidate's current friendships and support systems, what he or she thinks that people particularly appreciate in friendship with him or her, what he or she looks for in friends. You could also ask about any difficult relationships, how they have been coped with and what has been learnt from them. Starting with this far wider context you can then, eventually, move on to explore relationships within the particular context, perhaps work or church, where the negative assumption about relationships has come from.

In doing this you should have done justice to considering the issue and gained evidence to help you make a decision without having pointed to the source of your assumption. If your conclusions are negative the candidate should feel that they have been fairly reached rather than just being based on what a referee said. This will help to ensure that their relationship with the referee remains intact.

Gaining further experience or information

It may be that you need to explore issues in which the candidate doesn't have the necessary experience or understanding for you to be able to draw conclusions. In this case, suggest that they gain a particular experience, read a particular book, or do some research and write an assignment so that they gain the necessary experience or understanding for you to be able to explore the issues. It is experiences outside our comfort zone, followed by proper reflection, that can be of real value.

If this is necessary it is better, if at all possible, to suggest this reasonably early in the process, when you are still nurturing vocation, rather than in the final stages when you are testing vocation.

Selection not counselling

Helping candidates to discover information about themselves can take you very close to a counselling role, and two words of warning are required.

- If you are in the business of selection, you shouldn't be in the business of counselling. In the early stages of the process when the conversations are best described as an enquiry, there is a place for 'vocational' counselling; but for other forms of counselling candidates should be seeking help elsewhere, and not within the selection processes. When it becomes a 'testing' of vocation, rather than a 'nurturing' of vocation it is very confusing to try to mix the two roles up.
- If you are helping candidates to discover information about themselves that they were not previously aware of, then you might find that both you and the candidates are getting out of your depth. In such cases it is best to suggest that candidates speak to a professional counsellor who is used to working with people addressing such matters.

Keeping an open mind

Usually you will go into an interview with a brief to discuss particular issues and to come to a conclusion based upon your exploration. It is very easy, if you feel positive about the first couple of issues that you explore, to make up your mind and then only look for the positive in the rest of the interview. Of course, it's equally dangerous to come to negative conclusions with the first few topics and then to look for the worst in a person. It is amazingly easy to misunderstand what is being said and to draw the conclusions that you wish to, whether positive or negative.

If you are aware that certain issues are likely to produce particular responses in you, explore these issues last so that you remain as objective as possible for as long as possible. Investigating a difficult issue at the start is likely to cloud your judgement for the rest of the interview.

14

Using your faith: exploring faith issues

Exploring faith issues can be the topic area that produces the most heat and casts the least light. There are different reasons for this. With our limited human understanding, it is not easy to find words to do justice to our understanding of an infinite God. We cope with this by using different words and phrases to describe this understanding and relationship, and we do not always feel comfortable with the words that other Christians use. Our faith is based on our relationship with God and is something very intimate; someone else's faith journey, relationship with God and outworking of faith might be threatening to our own faith, assumptions and discipleship.

If I interview someone whose faith journey makes me feel very humble and inadequate, I may be left asking myself what right I have to ask questions of such a person. Alternatively, if I interview someone whose faith journey sounds very shallow and naïve, I may begin to question my own naivety. I may find myself asking how God can allow someone to draw certain conclusions from a particular biblical passage that is diametrically opposed to the conclusions that I have reached. Can they believe in the same God that I believe in? Surely my own conclusions cannot be wrong?

Reflect . . .

What are you trying to achieve in faith interviews? What is your priority in balancing:

- assent to particular doctrines?
- a particular understanding of mission and evangelism?
- integration of faith and life, or 'walking the talk'?

How can you begin to understand how someone is sustained, functions and grows as a Christian?

Difference and diversity

It is important that you acknowledge to yourself that your faith journey will have been different from the faith journey of the interviewee. You each have different personalities and different experiences of God and will have heard different teaching over the years. As a result of that you will experience God and respond to God in different ways. You may need to acknowledge this in front of God in prayer as you prepare for the interview, and you may need to acknowledge this in front of your fellow interviewers when you share your conclusions.

It can also be dangerous if, in contrast, your faith journey is very similar to the interviewee's. I have sometimes heard interviewers comment that they had a great time of fellowship with a candidate. The interview should not be a time of fellowship. There is a serious job to be done, and difficult issues to be explored. Interviewers should not be using the precious time available to share their own experiences; they need to be exploring the experiences of the interviewee.

Christian language

What word do you use to describe the second person of the Trinity? When someone talks about Jesus Christ then they will usually either talk of Jesus or of Christ; generally they will feel more comfortable with one of these words. While it is dangerous to stereotype, to some extent this might reflect an emphasis on a particular understanding of who Jesus Christ is. The word *Jesus* means *Joshua*, 'the one who saves', and is more readily identified with an understanding of a personal saviour. The term *Christ*, meaning *Messiah*, can be associated more with the cosmic Christ and a redeeming function that reaches out to the wider world, rather than focusing upon personal salvation.

What words do you use to describe the service involving bread and wine? Breaking Bread, the Eucharist, Holy Communion, the Liturgy, the Lord's Supper and the Mass are all terms that can be used. Some of these terms (arranged alphabetically rather than in any order of preference) can be identified with particular traditions within the Church.

Assuming that you have a regular time of prayer and Bible study, what term do you use to refer to this? You may use other words, but the terms 'quiet time' and 'Office' are two possibilities, and both would reflect different traditions within the Church.

It is easy to draw conclusions about where someone is coming from by the use of particular Christian words. It is also very easy to over-simplify and come to the wrong conclusions. If you use your own Christian vocabulary in the interview, it will be easy for the interviewee to make assumptions about where you are coming from, and what you would wish to hear. It can be very easy for the candidate to feed back the words that you think most appropriate.

What you need to try to do is to ask questions that do not use 'loaded' words and instead encourage interviewees to choose and use their own words. You are then in a position to feed their words back to them. If you ask interviewees to compare two different churches that they have belonged to, or even attended, they might use words such as evangelical, catholic, traditional, charismatic, liberal, middle-of-the-road, lively or dead. These words are all value judgements. As well as it being better if interviewees brings these words into the conversation and you then use their vocabulary, you can also ask them to describe what they mean by the use of that word. Similarly, if you ask about the type of service each Sunday at their church, then they are likely to talk about Communion, Eucharist, Mass and so on.

Doctrinal questions

As with doctrinal questions on application forms, I feel that asking doctrinal questions in an interview is not particularly helpful. If you ask people about the Trinity, it will remind them that they should be talking about the Father, Son and Holy Spirit in their answer. Instead, if you ask a more general question about their beliefs you can tell from their answer whether their faith is focused mainly around just one part of the Trinity. In particular, are one or two persons of the Trinity absent from all of their answers? If so, you may wish to explore their understanding of those persons of the Trinity that they have not referred to.

If you ask questions about 'man's state', you are likely to be given answers that mention fallen-ness, sin and the need for salvation, and how that salvation can only come through Jesus Christ. If you ask questions in other ways you will gain a more honest understanding of how the world is perceived and whether God is perceived to be at work in his world or not. In particular it can be helpful to ask what the 'gospel' or the 'good news' is for them. By asking what impact the existence of other faiths has upon their own faith, and going on to ask candidates to reflect upon comparisons between Christianity and other faiths, I have got candidates to talk about salvation and the uniqueness of the Christian revelation, without me introducing such words or phrases as salvation, sin, fallen-ness, uniqueness or man's state.

Faith and knowledge

A good way of finding out about someone's faith is to explore how firm a foundation it has. Is it built on solid experience or does it have a very shallow foundation? If the foundations are solid then faith will survive life's knock; if they are weak then faith can easily crack.

Certain questions will just skate around the surface of someone's faith. Ask why something is true and you might hear that the answer is because it says so in the Bible. But why is the Bible true? It says so in the book of Timothy. It would be just as easy to take the Qur'an as a starting point and prove anything mentioned there is true. If the candidate who argues in such a way then comes across something where the Bible might be more ambiguous, will his or her faith be able to cope, or will it all crack and come apart?

The answer that you probably want to hear is that personal experience of God has confirmed the biblical truth. People can argue with factual understandings and conclusions, but no one can take away personal experiences and the conclusions that have been reached as a result of such experience. It is this personal experience that will make the foundations of faith solid.

In English the verb *to know* can relate to a 'fact' or to a 'relationship' with a person. In many languages, including Hebrew and French, there are two distinct verbs. It is helpful to make this distinction in exploring faith issues: knowledge *about* God (faith and doctrine) is not the same as knowledge *of* God (a relationship with him and experience of him). The key is to find out how well the interviewee can make connections between facts about God and his or her experience of God.

Real life . . .

A student studying for a degree in theology had just come to a personal faith through a mission run by the Christian Union. Through the course of an interview it became apparent that her new faith did not yet allow her to make any sense of her study of theology. She was keeping her faith and her theology in separate boxes. Both were potentially damaging to each other; her theology had the potential to threaten her newly found faith, and her newly found faith questioned the assumptions that she needed to make in order to gain a good degree.

Exploring the connections between knowledge (factual understanding) and faith (personal experience) will help you to get beneath the surface of someone's faith and assess the foundations. There are a number of issues that can be explored and engaged with in order to establish this.

- Other Christian traditions and other denominations – is the interviewee able to show an appreciation for different Christian understandings?
- Christians of other cultures – can God only be understood within a particular culture, and will other understandings be threatening or enriching?
- Different styles of worship – can God be worshipped only in particular ways or will different styles of worship energize and excite the interviewee?
- Suffering – is there a theological understanding of suffering that ties in with experience? Be aware that a nice easy answer to this question may be of more concern than an admission of struggling with this issue. Is there any mention of God being present in any way within the suffering? Can the candidate express feeling, such as anger, to God, as the psalmist did? Can the candidate, like Job, question God? If everything has nice clear answers, will the candidate's faith be able to cope when the candidate, or

someone close to him or her, suffers terribly? Will his or her faith cope with ambiguity?

- Times of doubt – if people have already survived times of doubt they are likely to be able to survive them in the future. If they have never had any times of doubt it is harder to know whether they have the resources to face these in the future.

- Experiences of God within prayer life and how God does, or does not, answer prayer – if God has always answered the candidate's prayers then has the candidate kept his or her prayers at too safe a level?

- Contact with those of other faiths – it is worth exploring what the existence of other faiths says to the interviewee's own faith. Is the interviewee indifferent to the claims of others or does he or she see them as a challenge that might strengthen his or her own faith? As has been said, often it is the process of reflecting upon the claims of other faiths that allows a person to share what is at the real heart of his or her own faith.

- Relating faith to courses studied – some academic courses can be challenging to certain Christian beliefs. Christians that I have interviewed have had different understandings of creation and evolution. I am not concerned what their view is on this, but whether they are comfortable with their own understanding. I remember one biology student who believed in evolution within her course, but in a seven-day creation within her faith. She had no difficulty in keeping her faith and her studies in separate boxes. Some courses have an anti-Christian agenda and it is interesting to explore how Christians cope with this. As mentioned, studying theology can be quite challenging to faith.

- Relating faith to work – work can challenge faith in various ways. It might be the working practices rather than the end-product that really challenges some candidates. It can be interesting to explore what it means to be a Christian in certain places of work and also whether the 'vocation' to move into Christian work comes from giving in to the struggle of trying to be a Christian in the work place.

- Baptism – this is an issue that different Christians can have strong views on. Again, I am not so much interested in the conclusion as in the ability to understand the different perspectives and be able to relate their own experience logically, with a biblical understanding as well as an appreciation of a different perspective.

Other issues that might be worth exploring are:

- peace and reconciliation
- relating faith to political and social issues
- relating faith to moral and ethical issues
- women's leadership roles within the church
- human sexuality
- the authority of the Scriptures
- authority and fallen-ness within the church
- the charismatic movement
- Christian healing
- multi-faith worship.

Often there will be some current issue that is being debated in the Christian press, and it can be interesting to see whether this has been reflected upon and whether differing views on the subject have been taken into account or not.

Within some ministries, it will of course be important that the candidate does hold certain doctrinal views, but for most vocations the real question will be whether or not someone's faith is integrated; whether the candidate is able to make the connections between his or her factual understanding and his or her experience of God or relationship with God.

Faith, personality and teaching

Exploring some of the above issues might show that a candidate is living with uncertainty and does not have clear-cut answers to questions. If so, it can be valuable to explore how the candidate feels about not having definite answers. Often the answer to this will reflect the candidate's personality and the fact that some people can live more easily with uncertainties than others. It might be that the candidate's personality is happy with uncertainty, but his or her church teaching encourages certainty, or *vice versa*. In such cases it is definitely worth exploring whether the candidate is comfortable, and affirmed, in the answers being given and how this feels.

Whatever the answers to the above issues, it can be worth seeking how the interviewee copes with those who have different views.

In doing this, explore real situations that the interviewee has experienced rather than asking hypothetical questions.

What is also important, in such explorations, is whether it would be fair to put someone who is struggling with living with uncertainty into a situation where he or she would need to face more uncertainty.

Perhaps because I am comfortable with uncertainty, my own exploration of these issues will not be from a starting point that there are right or wrong answers, but that I want to see how interviewees are able to relate their own understanding to both their personal experience and their knowledge. (When I do this I need to remember not to let my body language or my choice of vocabulary indicate what answers I want to hear.)

Exploring spirituality

A spiritual journey

It is helpful to build up a picture of how people's faith has developed and how it has become personal to them rather than just reflecting the views of those who first nurtured the faith, be this family or friends. It is when people reach different conclusions from those who nurtured their faith that they really know that their faith is their own, rather than inherited.

Those who have been brought up within a Christian family might speak about specific episodes in childhood or their teens, perhaps a decision to be baptized or confirmed or a decision made at a Christian event that they would see as the starting point of their personal faith. However, I usually find that it is when they have moved away from the parental home that they have had to wrestle with the reality of their faith, and as a consequence that is when it has really become personal to them.

Sometimes people speak of three conversions: conversion to God, conversion to the world (that is, an awareness of God at work with his world) and conversion to the Church. The conversion to God may reflect the Trinitarian nature of God and there might be distinct steps in which the understanding of Father, Son and Holy Spirit has taken place. Certainly, when exploring the spiritual journey you should expect to find more than one key event or period.

What influences, people and books have shaped the candidate's spirituality? Are they all within a particular tradition or do they reflect diversity? If diversity, how is such diversity held together? Sometimes when interviewing those who hold together diversity, I have discovered that none of the traditions is fully understood and that the affirmation of diversity has been the result of shallowness; at other times it has been as the result of an amazing depth of spirituality.

Prayer life

Most candidates affirmed in a vocation are likely to move to a situation where they will not be receiving the same spiritual support as they did previously. It will therefore be important in the interview to explore their spiritual resources and their spiritual survival kit. What experience do they have of tapping into spiritual sustenance within a different context? The style and frequency of their prayer life will also be worth exploring. When does it not happen – is it when things are going badly or well? Is it when life is too busy, or when routine has been lost? Are there only limited styles of praying? Do they operate their prayer life only within a particular tradition or do they explore various spiritualities?

Again, it is helpful if you are not seeking right or wrong answers; you want to encourage honesty. It is better if your questioning implies that there will be dry times when a prayer life is not working or ceases. I will often start by saying, 'Tell me about your spiritual life' or, 'Tell me about your prayer life', then follow up by saying, 'Tell me about any dry periods' or, 'What will cause it not to be as regular as that?' If we have already identified difficult life experiences, I can ask more about where God was during those experiences. This will encourage the interviewee to discuss openly what was going on at such times.

Often the real growth occurs during such wilderness experiences and when a particular pattern of prayer ceases and is then succeeded, in due course, by a new pattern. If you interview someone who has been through dry periods and come through them, you can feel more confident that this person will come through a dry period in the future. If someone has never had such an experience, you have no evidence that he or she will be able to survive such a dry period in the future!

Bible study

Similarly, you will want to explore how someone reads and uses the Bible. Are certain sections always ignored, and if so, why? Have Bible reading resources been used? If so, are these changed from time to time to provide different insights? Often people will find that they need to stop one style of reading the Bible, and take a break, before they return to read the Bible with new enthusiasm and new tools to enhance their understanding.

Other issues

Other aspects of faith and spirituality that you might like to explore are listed below.

Faith sharing and mission:

- Is the candidate able to articulate what he or she believes and why? (Find out whether the candidate can do this in a way that sounds real, rather than reciting a well-rehearsed formula.)
- Does the candidate have experience of sharing his or her faith?
- How has the candidate tried to modify what is shared when relating his or her faith to different people with different world views and different aspirations? How does the candidate understand mission and what other mission activities has he or she been involved in?

Stewardship:

- What does Christian commitment say about the use of time, talents and money for the Kingdom?
- Does the outworking tie in with what is being said?

Guidance:

- How does the candidate understand God's calling?
- How does the candidate expect to be led by God?
- Does the candidate expect individual guidance or guidance through the wider body of Christ?
- How has the candidate seen God at work in the past when making important decisions?
- Has the candidate had to cope with thinking that God was saying one thing and then finding this was not so?

- Does the candidate believe that God only has one path for him or her?
- Does the candidate explain his or her sense of guidance in a way that sounds consistent and makes sense to him or her?

Interviewing clergy and the theologically trained

You may find yourself interviewing someone who has much more theological training than you. Often this can be a very positive and enriching experience, although you may become very aware of your own lack of knowledge. Sometimes questions about faith are given theological answers that will lose you. I have often had particular theologians' names given to me as answers to questions. In such cases I need to swallow my pride and remember that the purpose of the interview is for me to find out the information that I need, rather than for me to avoid showing how little theology I have studied. In a situation like this, push for a fuller answer, challenge the use of any Christian jargon and ask for an explanation in the interviewee's own words. One way to protect your integrity is not to say that you can't understand the answer but ask how the interviewee would explain the answer to someone who is not theologically trained!

Part 5
MAKING DECISIONS

15

Using your hands

The main way in which you will make use of your hands during the interview process is by writing notes in the interview itself and then writing these notes up as a report after the interview is over.

Making notes during the interview

As mentioned in Chapter 12, making a lot of notes during the interview may prevent you from listening properly. If you have a good memory, and have followed your interview plan (see Chapter 11), you may not need to write down much during the interview itself. This means you don't need to struggle with writing, listening and planning your next question all at the same time. When you look at the plan again later you should be able to remember what was said as you explored the different issues and the conclusions that you came to. If you went on to an issue that was not in the plan then you may well need to note it down to jog your memory when you write your report. Even if your memory is good it may be worth noting any exact details or dates that are particularly important. While writing too many notes may lead the candidate to think that you aren't listening carefully, you do want to find ways of reassuring the candidate that you are paying attention, and remembering what they have shared. Obviously, if you do not have a good memory, you will need to establish what level of note taking is necessary to recall the interview.

Real life . . .

An interview lasted for nearly three hours and the interviewer, with an excellent memory, didn't make a single note! The interviewee wondered how the interviewer could possibly remember all of the relevant facts that he had shared. He understandably wondered if nothing he had said was valuable enough to be written down!

If you are not writing down notes, your hands can be tempted to play with the papers. If you spend a lot of time shuffling through the candidate's papers it can appear that you are more interested in reading what has already been written, rather than hearing what is being said. As mentioned on p. 127, if you need to check a detail, don't be afraid to explain what you are doing.

Remember to think about your own body language and, if you aren't writing notes or holding papers, do occasionally observe what you are doing with your hands.

Immediately after the interview

Shortly after the interview try to write some brief notes, or headings, to prompt your memory. If issues that were not on your plan were explored make a note of them, along with any details that you might forget.

Writing the report

Sometimes, time dictates that you need to write your report immediately, but if possible allow some time so that you can mull it over and so that the Holy Spirit can help you to notice connections and patterns. Don't, however, leave writing the report for so long that you forget things, and if you are interviewing more than one person you'll have to be very careful not to muddle the candidates up!

How you actually go about writing the report will depend on various different factors.

Where does the report come in the selection process?

Reflect . . .

What is the purpose of your interview report?

First of all you need to establish clearly in your mind what the purpose of your interview was, and consequently, what the purpose of the report you are writing is. As mentioned in Chapter 5, the purposes of the selection process may be to:

- test vocation to a specific agency;
- ascertain an appropriate time scale;
- determine factors influencing suitable locations;
- identify training needs;
- identify pastoral needs;
- identify spiritual needs; and
- affirm the candidate as a Christian loved and valued by God.

Any interview report should feed into the aims that you have identified for your own selection processes. So, for example, is your report to gain information that will decide whether the candidate should go any further through the processes? Is it to provide information to help within the final decision-making process?

Reports that are written during the earlier stages of selection can helpfully flag up questions that need to be explored by others at a later stage. If the interviewer was briefed to explore a particular issue then the report should include conclusions on this, and the other interviewers will not need to go over the same ground.

At the final selection stage, if at all possible, reports have to relate clear decisions and judgements about the specific topics that have been explored. They should only be giving new information and clarifying issues, not repeating information from earlier reports. At this stage it is not helpful to raise questions for further exploration. These interviews also need to identify parameters that have an impact upon location and to identify training, pastoral and spiritual issues that need to be borne in mind within the ongoing processes. Clearly, different types of reports are needed to fulfil these different tasks.

As discussed in Chapter 10, your own background and agenda can impinge upon the interview, so it can be helpful to give an opening comment based on perceptions of how the interview appeared to go for both you and the interviewee.

The Data Protection Act

Every interviewer should be aware of who may read the report. Although this will obviously include other members of the selection panel, the Data Protection Act means any candidate has the right to ask to see their file and read any interview report that is held on it. As mentioned above (see p. 81), this means candidates can also see any references that are held on file. You should ensure that you, and your organization, are familiar with the Data Protection Act and develop policies on the recording of data, to fulfil your obligations under the law. Develop guidelines as to what information is stored, why it is stored, how it is stored and who has access to it, and also who has access to any specifically sensitive information. Related to the question of why it is stored, you will also need to determine how long such information is kept for, and how any information shared with others is retrieved and destroyed.

I was familiar with a process in which, if someone was invited for an interview and didn't accept the offer, we would hold the application papers for a further six to 12 months. If the person had been interviewed and was invited to the next stage, we held the papers for a further two to three years. At one level, you may feel that if you have not selected a candidate then you do not need to keep the information any longer. But if there might be an appeal against your decision then you do need that information. You may feel it is appropriate to hold such information for several months, perhaps even a few years, before you shred the papers. Having established a practice, it is important to check papers every six months so that papers can be shredded as necessary.

If you have created a selection process in which candidates are reassured that you have their interests at heart, then they are unlikely to ask to see their file or read interview reports. In order to gain this trust, make it clear beforehand why you need information and what you will do with it. At the end of interviews say what happens next, and who will see interview reports, and why. If you are recording particularly sensitive information, discuss with the candidate how and why this is recorded and agree together how such sensitivities should be handled.

As people become more aware of their right to see information that is held on them you may well find more candidates asking to see their reports. If someone does ask to see the file it is unlikely to be someone for whom everything has been straightforward! Each and every interview report must be written on the understanding that the interviewee might read it.

Style of the report

The type of report will depend upon the style and purpose of selection process that you are involved in and what is expected from each interview report. It is helpful to think in terms of two distinct styles of report: narrative reports and judgemental reports.

Narrative reports

During preliminary stages it is helpful to produce long narrative reports. These will record what has been said about various issues, but allow the reader to make decisions and decide whether or not the candidate should be considered further and what type of location might best fit. The reports themselves avoid making judgements or, at least, they avoid making negative judgements. You might wish to make positive judgements and comment and then raise questions for further discussion, or even just allow the narrative to speak for itself. The narrative (what the candidate told you) is information that is known, whereas your judgements are assumptions, and questions are ways of seeking greater clarity (see the selection strategy window on p. 49).

Judgemental reports

At the final selection stage, interviewers need to be make decisions and judgements about the candidate. Because the official report on file can be read by the candidate it can be helpful to ask the interviewers to produce 'working documents'. These 'working documents' can then be used to make a decision and to produce a conference report to go in the candidate's file. The working document can then be shredded. The interviewers are free to make judgements and then the reports can be written up by someone in the organization with responsibility for making sure that the reports are written in an acceptable manner. Although the interview report for the file is not written in a narrative form, there will need to be enough evidence in the report to back up any negative judgement. The decision and judgements should have been based on information that the candidate shared and discussed with the interviewer, and the candidate should feel that the process has therefore been fair.

Why a written report?

The discipline of writing a report forces you to process the information that you gleaned from the interview. It is only when forced to express your conclusions that you will begin to clarify and formulate fully your thoughts and opinions.

It is helpful to encourage the interviewers to read aloud their interview reports, or working documents, to the others on the selection committee. There are two good reasons for this: the first is that a written report is usually briefer than the oral report that begins, 'I won't read this, to save time I will just pick out the helpful bits . . .' Usually, when someone tries to do this, they jump around and come back to issues and add details that they have not written down, and take twice as long as if they had read a written report.

The second reason is that reading a written report encourages all the interviewers to stick with their own conclusions. Sometimes you will find that your conclusions are different from those of the other interviewers. If this is the case then it is important that you stick to your original conclusions rather than feel that you need to say what everybody else is saying.

What not to include in a report

Occasionally your interview might reveal very sensitive information that, although it needs noting, is best not recorded within an interview report that has a wider readership. In such cases I have kept a more general reference to issues in the interview report and put fuller details in an envelope marked 'Strictly Confidential' and made sure that I have shared the contents of the envelope only when it has been absolutely necessary. I have also explained to the candidate how I was handling this sensitivity, discussing who did need full access, and why, and have gained the candidate's agreement to this practice. The nature of what might be considered so sensitive might vary with different agencies, but it is worth establishing your own practice as to what is done with particularly sensitive, confidential areas and to decide how information is recorded and kept on information related to:

- abuse – physical, emotional or sexual
- addictions – to soft or hard drugs, alcohol or pornography, and as evidenced by eating disorders, and so on
- criminal activity
- circumstances leading to divorce
- family relationships, where there have been difficulties and breaks in relationships
- marital problems
- psychiatric problems
- homosexuality
- sexual relationships outside marriage and
- suicide attempts.

With some of these issues, you may wish to seek professional psychiatric advice to help you within your decision-making processes. To help the professionals in their task of assessing the situation, you need to pass on the information that you have discovered, filed separately as being 'strictly confidential'.

Making a recommendation

A question that interviewers might ask is whether they should make a recommendation at the end of their report; after all they have only explored certain issues and not gained the whole picture. If the interviewers have been asked to look into particular topics, they should have been able to make judgements about each specific issue before moving on to explore the next. As such, they should be in a position to make a judgement based on the issues that they have explored. This might mean making a positive judgement on certain issues and being less positive on others.

Interviewers are not in a position to make a judgement on the issues that they have not explored. If they make a positive judgement on the issues that they have explored and other interviewers make different decisions based on the issues that they have explored, this does not mean that someone got it right and someone else got it wrong; it means that each has made a decision based on the issues that the wider group asked him or her to explore.

16

Making and giving decisions

When you are nurturing vocation then at each stage you will need to decide whether to proceed, whether to conclude the process or whether to ask the candidate for further work or reflection before making a decision.

When you are testing vocation you will need, at the end of the process, to make a selection decision. The style of the decision-making process will, rightly, vary for each organization but there are certain issues worth reflecting upon when considering the decision-making process.

Obviously, the process needs to fulfil the purpose of your selection strategy, as mentioned in Chapter 5, but it may also need to inform other decisions such as the actual role or location of the vocation, any training the candidate may require, and the level and type of pastoral and spiritual support that the candidate needs for the vocation to be successful. If so, a process should be designed to enable these functions to be achieved.

What are the possible decisions?

It's a good idea to develop a set of guidelines about what decisions may be made at the end of the process. This will ensure that everyone involved is working within the same parameters and it should also ensure that the candidates are given clear information.

Yes

If you want to accept the candidate into your organization, you might consider the following possible decisions.

- A straightforward 'yes' – this is unlikely, since usually there will be provisions or conditions attached.
- Provisionally selected or selected for training – for many vocations, selection will be considered either as provisional or as

selection for training. The positive selection decision is allowing the candidate to commence a period of training, and the person is then finally accepted into the vocation after successfully completing the training period.

Yes, provided that . . .

You may accept the candidate, but conditionally on one or more of the following types of factors.

- Subject to references – increasingly, within the secular world, references are called for only after a post has been conditionally offered. When testing vocation, you will, it is hoped, have gathered references at a much earlier stage in the process (see p. 142) so that the interviewers can use the information gained as an integral part of the interview process. Having said that, there can easily be occasions when not all of the references have arrived before the final interviews. In such cases, the selectors will need to decide whether they have gained enough evidence to make a final decision anyway, or whether their acceptance is still subject to their receiving the final references and feeling positive about these. In such circumstances, there will be a need to establish who has the task of deciding whether the references are satisfactory and what would need to be done by whom if the references raise issues that need further investigation.

- Subject to medical report – if medical clearance is needed but has not been obtained before the final selection, then this fact must be acknowledged within the selection decision.

- Subject to suitable location – mission agencies, in particular, are unlikely to take candidates through a selection process if they are not confident that there will be a suitable location at the end of the process, but a location that appears feasible at the start of the selection process may not still be viable by the time a decision has been made or after the training has been completed. Circumstances may have changed, making the location inappropriate or unsafe; suitable housing or children's schooling may be unavailable at a realistic cost; a visa or work permit may no longer be obtainable; or another agency may have filled the opening. Although there is often a 'Holy Spirit factor' so that a new and more appropriate door opens to replace the door that has closed, this cannot be guaranteed.

- Subject to child protection screening – if you have included such screening within your processes and the clearance has not come through before the selection event, then this should be acknowledged within the decision.
- Subject to finance – increasingly, Christian agencies are struggling to find money in a challenging financial climate and many expect the candidate to take some, or all, of the responsibility for the necessary fundraising. The selection decision might need to be conditional until the candidate and agency are convinced that the funding will materialize.
- Subject to certain experiences or qualifications – sometimes an 'in-principle' decision can be made, but there will still be the need for an anticipated qualification or an experience to be gained, and reflected on before the conditional selection can be confirmed.

Ideally, selection should happen after as many as possible of the conditions have been achieved, but this is not always possible. What is not helpful is for a 'yes' decision to be given but with so many caveats that realistically it is a 'no' rather unkindly dressed up as a 'yes'. It may make the decision-makers feel better to say 'yes', but they are only fooling themselves and causing additional pain if a 'yes' has conditions attached to it that are unlikely to be met.

If substantial training is part of the process anyway, it can sound attractive to the decision-makers to insist upon certain things being addressed or achieved during training. But it is not helpful for candidates to leave a job and begin training if there is a strong possibility that they will be told during this time that the conditions have not been met and that consequently they are not selected. Such a decision can also be very difficult for the others on the training course to cope with and whose sympathies will, generally, be with their fellow student.

With any conditional selection, it needs to be clear, both to the selectors and to the candidate:

- when the conditions need to be met by;
- who is responsible for monitoring progress and determining whether the conditions have been met; and
- what will happen if they are not fully met.

No, not at this point in time

Sometimes there will be a desire to give a decision that comes between a conditional 'yes' and an absolute 'no'. While not being prepared to say 'yes', there may be recognition of the candidate's potential, and a desire to affirm that potential.

You might consider responding to this dilemma by giving a 'not yet' decision. Unfortunately, by saying 'not yet' you may be implying that there will eventually be a time when the answer will be 'yes'. By doing this, you are setting up expectations that you cannot necessarily meet. You are on slightly safer ground saying 'no, not at this point in time'. Such a decision does acknowledge that decisions are made at a particular point in time and leaves the question open as to whether circumstances will be different at some time in the future.

But even with 'no, not at this point in time' decisions, candidates can be keen to know what they need to do in order to come back and gain a 'yes' decision. If the question had been as easy as this, you could probably have given a 'conditional yes' instead. If it is just a matter of gaining a qualification or a particular experience, the 'conditional yes' is probably a more appropriate decision. 'No, not at this point in time' might be used when an issue needs to be satisfactorily addressed and a particular formula that will make this happen cannot be guaranteed.

I can think of a couple of examples when my organization concluded that we did not have enough evidence of an ability to cope with a cross-cultural situation to make a 'yes' decision. In saying 'not at this point in time', we were suggesting that if such experience was gained for a few months we could explore the issue again. In these cases, there was clear guidance as to what needed to be done so that we could explore the issue again later. We were careful to clarify that a 'yes' decision was not conditional upon the experience being gained, but that the experience was necessary for us to explore the issue fully before making a final decision.

Often the 'not at this point in time' answer does beg the question as to what needs to be done for a 'yes' decision to be forthcoming. Part of the real answer might be 'getting on with life and seeing if there is still a strong sense of calling in the future'.

Appeals and further applications

In a large enough organization, it might be possible to establish an appeal process, but in a situation where the 'gate' for the selection process is focused in one person then it is impossible to set up an appeal system that could be completely objective. If you do establish such a process you will need to determine whether a process can be objective, when candidates are informed of this and how long they need to wait before beginning the appeal. It is not helpful for candidates to return through processes if they are feeling damaged from the first process.

Who are the decision-makers?

Often full-time staff will conduct preliminary interviews at the nurturing stage and facilitate the final testing of selection, but the final selection interviews are conducted by appointed volunteers or committee members representing the wider Body of Christ. Because they have not had previous contact with the candidates they will bring an objectivity to the process that might be lacking in those who have nurtured the vocation and got to know the candidates over a period of time. It is important to be clear as to which people, of those present in the room when decisions are being made, are actually party to the decision-making process and which are there purely as facilitators.

If not all of those involved in the decision-making process have interviewed each of the candidates then it is important to clarify whether they are all equals within the decision-making process for each candidate or whether the voices of those who interviewed the candidate should carry more weight.

Does everyone present have a full set of papers? If so, have they all read them in detail? If not everyone present has access to the same evidence, then this does need to be borne in mind in giving weight to their comments when decisions are made.

Making decisions

During the nurturing stage it will often be one person – the one who has just interviewed the enquirer – making the decision whether to proceed to the next stage, whether there is the need for further work before proceeding or whether the process should come to an end. Sometimes this decision will be made there and then and sometimes there will be time for prayerful reflection and/or discussion with others before decisions are made.

At final selection, when you are testing vocation, it is important to have clear procedures so that the processes are seen to be transparent.

As I have stressed throughout this book, I feel that it is important that decisions are made not only from evidence, but from evidence based on information that both the interviewers and the candidate are aware of. I believe that the interviewers should go into the interviews with a clear brief of what they need to consider, although being open to exploring other issues that might surface if they have not yet been looked into and are not going to be discussed by other interviewers.

It is very helpful to have short interviewers' meetings between the interviews. These should not be a time of passing on opinions, but of sharing 'the sins of trespass and omission'. If you have strayed onto another interviewer's brief, then that interviewer should be informed. If you have omitted to explore an issue that you should have covered, then someone else can be asked to investigate it. If a comment from the candidate has made you think that something else needs exploration, another interviewer can be asked to follow this up.

If in the decision-making process the interviewers read aloud their reports (see above) they should do so uninterrupted; there will be opportunities later, when they have said their piece, for others to question them. As the selection process can be a time when the candidate processes ideas, it is helpful to listen to interview reports about a candidate in the order in which the interviews occurred. By hearing the interview reports chronologically, you will gain an idea of the way that the candidate's thinking has progressed. Interviewers should be encouraged to be concise in delivering their reports and sometimes, after they have read their report, they should be asked to clarify or justify their comments or conclusions.

If any of those who have not interviewed have a significant contribution to make it could come at this point. It is not helpful to bring intuitive comments at this point, when it is too late to explore issues further; so such contributions do need to be based on evidence.

When all the reports have been read the person chairing the meeting can then enable a discussion about the candidate. Below, I outline a possible process that could be used as the basis for decision-making, not only as a way of gaining the evidence needed for the different aspects of the selection process, but also as a way of knowing what to say to candidates who are not accepted. It also provides a helpful template during the nurturing stages of the process.

Although I argued in Chapter 1 that a vocation, or call, to the ministry is essential, I do believe that the other criteria mentioned here are part of assessing that vocation. There's no point in starting by affirming a vocation only to come to negative conclusions about the other questions! I find the order expressed below helpful.

1 Can the candidate make a positive contribution to the ministry that you have in mind? To answer this will require consideration of family circumstances; professional skills; an understanding of, and 'heart' for, the ministry; appropriate people skills and sensitivity to the culture that the ministry will be within; and a reasonable match with your selection criteria, job description or competencies. If the ministry is seen as a long-term one then the consideration should include the person's ability to make a long-term contribution. If the answer is no, you need to explain, from the evidence that you have gathered, the reasons why you can't go ahead, but encourage the person with concrete suggestions to use his or her skills and gifts in other ways.

2 Does the candidate fit the ethos of your church or agency? This should be an issue identified at an early stage in the process, rather than at final selection. If the interview process reveals that the candidate doesn't, after all, fit your ethos, then you will want to explain the reasons why you cannot go ahead and encourage the candidate to consider a church or agency that has an ethos where he or she does fit. Again it is helpful to give concrete suggestions that affirm gifts but say how the gifts might be used with a church or agency that provides a better match.

3 From what you know about possible openings and locations for the ministry, do you feel confident that the candidate will be placed after training? If there are uncertainties then there is the need to be open about these and make sure that the candidate

is fully in the picture before giving up a job or selling a house to begin training. If you are not likely to be able to find a suitable opening or location, then explain the reasons why you can't go ahead and encourage the candidate to consider a church or agency that is likely to have a suitable location.

4 Do you and the candidate believe that he or she is called to serve in this ministry with your organization? Is there some understanding of call to mission or ministry, rather than a task-based approach working from a match of skills? As mentioned above, people express a call in very different ways, but can the candidate articulate a sense of calling that is real for him or her? Do you, despite differences and barriers of vocational language, feel that the candidate is called to this ministry? If not, explain that, despite the candidate being an appropriate person with appropriate skills, a vocation or call to your ministry is an essential criterion and that you don't believe that he or she is called by God to this work at this time. To do this effectively, you may need to repeat back what you have heard the candidate say and explain how this doesn't constitute a vocation. Encourage the candidate to use his or her gifts in other ways and to reflect upon his or her sense of leading.

Once you have answered these questions, you will need to see which of the decision outcomes outlined above best fits.

- If the answer to all of the above questions is yes, then you can move ahead and give one of the 'yes' answers as outlined above.
- If the only 'no' is based on a lack of a suitable opening or location, then the candidate could be given a conditional acceptance as long as the serious concerns about the likelihood of finding a suitable location are stressed and clearly heard, and as long as the candidate realizes that he or she should not make any irreversible decisions until there is greater clarity.
- If the candidate has the fit with your ethos, but either does not yet have the skills or maturity or does not have the sense of call, then it may be appropriate to give a 'not at this point in time' decision. If it is an offer for a long-term ministry, and you are able to offer short-term possibilities, then it may be appropriate to point towards these ministries as a way of either developing the skills and maturity or developing the call.

Having made a decision to proceed, then the selection process is also an opportunity to consider the following questions.

- Are there parameters to be taken into account in considering suitable locations?
- Are there specific learning needs?
- Are there pastoral needs that should be noted?
- Are there spiritual needs that should be noted?

Monitoring the effectiveness of decision-making

In time, it becomes possible to reflect upon the validity of the decisions that have been made in the past. If candidates are being selected for training then it will be valuable to revisit the factors that led to someone being selected whose vocation was not confirmed at the end of the training period. Having said this, it is perhaps true that some of those who go on to a very creative ministry have struggled with the structures of training.

The real measure of how effective a selection process is will be how effective a ministry candidates goes on to have. Often it may be many years before this can really be determined.

Taking risks

If a selection process was to be considered as being 'so good' that it didn't select anyone whose selection didn't raise questions at some point, then the likelihood would be that the process had also turned down some good people. Our Christian calling is not meant to be risk-free and I believe that we are corporately called to take some risks within our decision-making. A consideration of the 12 disciples (see p. viii) shows that God works through all people, including those who might be deemed 'unsuitable', but this needs to be held in tension with the damage that a bad decision can have upon not only the person selected but also a community.

I can think of some examples of someone's calling for overseas mission being affirmed but when, ultimately, it has not worked out for the person and he or she has needed to return. Usually the factors leading to this have been identified at selection, but the selection decision had either been seen as a risk worth taking or the location was inappropriate for such risks, either because of changing circumstances, or because location parameters had not been taken fully into consideration. Both scenarios provide opportunities for learning and evaluation within the selection processes.

Real life . . .

A candidate was turned down by one particular mission agency but then went on to become an internationally famous missionary serving independently. Was the original agency wrong to turn her down?

No. She would never have fitted in with their organization and the constraints she would have had to operate under there. She was only to realize her full potential through another channel. The responsibility of the first agency was to say 'no' in such a way that she was not damaged or diverted from her true calling.

How are decisions given?

If at all possible, when nurturing vocation, give an oral decision as to what the next stage should be at the end of the interview. Of course, you might need to consult with others, but you could still outline the likely conclusion and the reasons why.

If you have a residential process you could also consider giving oral decisions at the final selection process. Of course, time constraints may make this impossible and it would be cruel to invite someone to return and see you, perhaps asking them to travel many miles, only to say no, you do not wish to affirm their vocation. It is, however, worth considering some of the benefits of oral decisions, if only to reflect upon whether such benefits can be achieved in other ways.

Verbal decisions provide a good discipline for the selection processes:

- practically, they allow important follow-up about what will happen next with training and ongoing contact; and
- pastorally, they allow you to gain some perception as to how decisions are received and what has, and has not, been heard.

More significantly I believe that it has an impact upon how decisions are expressed, and possibly the nature of the decision itself. In giving a negative decision, it is all very well to express feelings, opinions and hypotheses that someone else needs to pull together and express within a formal letter. Knowing that one or two of the interviewers will be involved in giving the decision, face to face, certainly sharpens the mind. It makes the selectors aware that they need to give decisions that are primarily evidence-based. Decisions need to be made from the material that is known by the candidate as well as the interviewers, rather than from material based on assumptions rather than knowledge or from things that the interviewers know but the candidate doesn't.

If you don't have such evidence, it is difficult to give a negative decision with integrity. If you are only left with feelings then you might need to arrange a further interview to get the further evidence that is needed to make a decision. The candidates will have given much as they have come through the selection processes; we owe it to them to give credible, evidence-based, decisions.

Giving a decision orally, whether positive or negative, is an opportunity to clarify what has been heard and what has not been heard. During all of the emotional ups and downs of the culmination of the selection process, it is easy for miscommunication. It is helpful to suggest that candidates repeat back what they have heard said; this gives an opportunity to correct any misunderstandings. The oral decision should also be followed up with a letter so that what has been said is in writing as well.

Usually with a difficult decision it is helpful to use two interviewers to relay the decision. The dynamics of this needs consideration or else there can be opportunities for greater confusion and hurt. This works best if one interviewer actually gives the decision and the other one tries to observe the dynamics, and work out if there is any miscommunication going on. Definitely avoid any sense of 'good cop, bad cop' with one giving all the bad news and the other being positive and affirming.

I am aware that, for practical reasons, many organizations need to give decisions by letter. Even so, it could be a helpful discipline to use in a written decision only words that you would have been prepared to have given face to face. Failing this you could consider a phone call, or following up a letter with a phone call.

What is said?

In the section on making a decision, I have given some clues as to what can be said to those whom you do not take forward. It is essential that any decision is positive and affirming of the candidates, valuing all that they have experienced of God within their lives, all that they have to offer and affirming that they are loved and accepted by God. Ironically, if we are accepting people it is easier to mention failings than if we are not accepting people. As long as a candidate is being accepted and affirmed within the vocation that they are exploring, they will happily hear and take on board the areas that they need to work on.

When giving negative decisions you do not need to list every fault, but you do need to focus upon the ones that are key to your making the decision. It is essential that you are focusing upon reasons where you know that you have evidence to back up your conclusions.

It is preferable when giving decisions to use 'corporate' and 'definite' language: 'we have concluded . . .' rather than 'I think . . .' or 'I feel . . .'. By doing this you are indicating that it is a corporate decision and not one you have made yourself, and that it is a conclusion, a final decision, rather than a personal thought or feeling that is negotiable.

Who is it said to?

When you do say 'no' to people, particularly at the final stage of the processes, there will often be the need for effective pastoral follow-up, so that the candidate can deal with pain and grief and be encouraged within an appropriate timescale to explore other, more appropriate, channels to use his or her gifts and skills for the Kingdom. This is best carried out locally, usually by the local church. Generally it is not helpful for the processes that have said 'no' to try to give ongoing pastoral support; it can easily create an unhealthy dependency that can lead to further pain.

With the candidate's permission, it can be helpful to inform the church of the decision and the reasons behind it, but whether this is done by letter or by a phone call might depend upon personal preference and also upon the level of involvement that the church had in the earlier parts of the process.

Wrestling with God

In Genesis 32.22–32 we read the story of Jacob wrestling with God. I believe that all those who begin to explore a vocation are invited to wrestle with God.[23] Jacob comes away from the wrestling match with a dislocated hip but also a blessing from God. Those suffering from a dislocated hip can limp and show off their pain, or they can face the brief, but more intense, pain of the healing process. If you can help candidates to discover what their true vocation is, and if you are able to clearly identify to candidates the reasons why you cannot accept them, carefully enough for them to hear and understand your reasons then, despite the experience of pain, they can begin to address and deal with these issues and become more fully the person that God wants them to be. As such, you can be part of the process that brings God's blessing upon their lives.

This book is written in the hope that it helps you to be an agent of God's blessing on those you meet as they wrestle with God in exploring their vocation. Jesus promises us the gift of the Holy Spirit so that we enter into our involvement in nurturing and testing vocation knowing that we do so not only as part of the Body of Christ but also confident that, despite our own failings, the Holy Spirit is there in the process as well. For me, the corporate engagement in this task with others, who are different from myself and challenge my views, as well as the privilege of having an excuse to probe deeply into the exciting stories of how God has been at work in the life of others, has been a great blessing to my own life and vocation.

Notes

1 Francis Dewar, *Called or Collared?* SPCK, London, 1991, pp. 2–3.
2 Stuart Buchanan, *On Call*. BRF, Abingdon, 2001; now out of print. Copies of the BRF edition are available from CMS <http://www.cms-shop.org.uk/mall/productpage.cfm/CMS/_184101-2157/85955/On%20Call>. It is also available as a free-downloadable resource on the St John's Nottingham website <http://www.stjohns-nottm.ac.uk/page/show/163/> Chapter 2 – Set aside by the Body of Christ.
3 *On Call*, Chapter 2 – An ongoing process.
4 Margaret Silf, *Landmarks: An Ignatian Journey*. Darton, Longman and Todd, London, 1998.
5 *Landmarks*, p. 77.
6 *Landmarks*, pp. 77–9.
7 John Adair, *How to Find Your Vocation*. Canterbury Press, Norwich, 2000.
8 Ian Aveyard and David Muir, *Fit for the Purpose*. St John's Extension Studies, Nottingham, 1997.
9 *On Call*, Chapter 8 – How does God move people?
10 *On Call*, Chapter 7 – Enabling others.
11 This thinking is developed in an article by Stuart Buchanan, 'You called me?' published in *The Reader* in February 2002.
12 Lesslie Newbigin, *The Good Shepherd*. Mowbray, London, 1984.
13 *On Call*, Chapter 4 – Growth in relationships.
14 *On Call*, Chapter 5 – Products of our culture.
15 Richard Tiplady, ed., *Postmission*. Paternoster Press, Carlisle, 2002, pp. 58–9.
16 *Postmission*, p. 27.
17 Richard Burridge, *Four Gospels, One Jesus?* SPCK, London, 1994, p. 25, p. 164.
18 For a fuller understanding see Stuart Murray, *Post-Christendom*. Paternoster Press, Carlisle, 2004.
19 There are certainly exceptions to this trend and some very encouraging growth noted in the UK within many Anglican cathedral congregations as well as among the Orthodox.
20 <http://feweb.uvt.nl/center/hofstede/page3.htm>.
21 Vincent Donovan, *Christianity Rediscovered*. SCM Press, Norwich, pp. 28–9.
22 William D. Taylor, ed., *Too Valuable to Lose*. William Carey Library Publishers, Pasadena, California, USA, 1997.
23 For more on this see *On Call*, Chapter 3 – Wrestling with God.

Index